Ask Dave Again:

MORE Usable Answers to Business Questions

David Conrad, Ed.D.

Heuristic Books

Saint Charles Missouri

USA

Copyright 2015

ISBN 978-1-59630-096-5

LCCN 2015946196

Published, 2015

Heuristic Books

is an imprint of

Science & Humanities Press

63 Summit Pointe
Saint Charles MO 63301-0571
636-394-4950
Heuristicbooks.com

Heuristic Books

for Mathematics & Management Science
heuristicbooks.com

Book Dedication

To my wonderful family
of whom I could write a book of thanks.

Foreword

I just finished reading "Ask Dave Again" and couldn't wait to share my thoughts. I have read a number of management and leadership self-help books and this one is a gem; it provides advice that is practical, highly useful, and applicable to numerous current business challenges. It could just as easily be called, "How to survive and thrive in any organization."

From Dave's credentials as a business person, professor, and scholar, it is obvious that he has studied the theories of leadership and management, and his writing makes it apparent he has reflected on them in the context of his own experiences. I like the way he sets up the cases (some bordering on playful rants), drawing on his experiences generated from both good bosses and bad bosses, toxic employees, and from effective and ineffective leaders.

Dave's writing style makes it clearly apparent he has been both an employee and a manager in a number of non-academic endeavors and has suffered the bumps and bruises that result in just, plain trying to do a job. I know his career is littered with some serious mistakes – that he and others have made – but he has learned from them and chooses to help others by offering the best, straight-forward advice he can possibly give. It is apparent that he is proud of the many management initiatives he has undertaken and the victories he has achieved.

The format of answering questions from readers in a "Dear Abby-like" approach provides an effective platform for the practical, while providing the ability to incorporate academic, real world and theoretical logic. It is refreshing, because he actually suggests specific, implementable actions to take, or offering alternatives one could choose. The format also allows the reader to debate his suggestions, and hopefully, use the recommendations to tailor their own specific approach to resolving a problem. The book did provide me with a couple, "come on, really?" moments for some self-debate and idea generation on my own. Maybe that is the point of the book: you consider what he says, but you have to make the final call.

A seasoned manager reading the book will see themselves in the examples from the perspective of the good, the bad, and the ugly of organizations and the management of them. It drew me back to personal situations I would rather forget, but allowed me to analyze the "if I could do it over" options. A new manager or manager "wannabes" just entering the management "game" will get some insight into the common business challenges that will allow them to get a leg up on the "what would I do if..." situations that all managers encounter. Both small business owners/managers and large corporation managers will find his insights useful and self-reflecting, while providing a base for taking action, getting results, and achieving self-improvement.

So, after saying all that, I am going to buy each of my employees a copy of the book.

Dr. George Dierberger, Ed.D.

Assistant Professor of Business, Augsburg College

Minneapolis, Minnesota

Contents

Introduction

My personal mission is, "To rid the world of bad management." I mean to broaden this by including bad leadership, because I believe good managers are and should be good leaders and good leaders – people will throw stones at me for stating this – should be good managers. To accomplish this, I realize I have to first know what bad management and bad leadership is. It appears it is all around me; I just need to open my eyes and recognize it for what it is. Further, maybe I can help others recognize it and, more importantly, constructively deal with it without committing career suicide.

I wrote this book for that very purpose. I have suffered under tyrants, autocrats, malicious and hurtful, and downright incompetent managers. To be fair, I have also served under and learned from managers that I will call true inspirational leaders. This latter group was composed of selfless, dedicated, relationship-oriented, and respectful folks, who just knew how to talk to people and understand and deliver what they want and need.

I also wrote this book to help workers better understand their colleagues and coworkers – as well as their managers - and to live and work with them to be productive, innovative, and collegial, not as adversarial, mistrusting foes. Work is often a strange environment and we seem to put on our "work faces," which make us think and act far differently from the way we act in our personal lives. If people are people, we need

1

to treat and interact with them as people always and everywhere. I try to propose ways to do this.

The organizational problems and challenges of the past still haunt us today, and probably will for decades to come. We seem to lack good communication skills. This is made evident by the zillions of studies done, where respondents say, "Our communication stinks." Or, in so many words. We have strategy, planning, and implementation problems. We have rewards and recognition problems. We have hiring and development problems. And we have coworkers we just plain do not get along with each other. Most people would say that, these are management and leadership problems, because they should be managed and solved by leadership. You know what I say, "Correct!" If management/leadership were doing their job, these problems would be mitigated and taken care of.

My claim to fame is that, I have answers, but I don't know everything – what a revelation. I do my best to carefully read what others are asking me, to pause, reflect, and analyze the implications and repercussions, and to "thoughtfully" come up with what I term, "whole systemic, implementable, and measurable solutions." Thank you very much! In any case, you can be the judge and determine if what I have to say has value to address the questions posed. So, on to Chapter One!

Chapter 1 – Those Darn Coworkers

This is nothing new, but difficult people exist at work as in all facets of life, and they come in every size and variety. Dealing with some types is easier when the person is just generally obnoxious, or when their behavior affects more than one person. But it is much tougher when they personally attack you or undermine your professional work, reputation, and standing in either direct or passive-aggressive styles.

While you probably can't change such people, the good news is that there are tips for dealing with problem people in the workplace – basically, you can make conscious choices to ignore and rise above them, and avoid being their victim.

I know I have worked with truly outstanding coworkers in the past – the ones who are cheerful, helpful, and are as nice as nice can be. I don't have tips for working with these people; I just advise you to enjoy their work and company, and be nice to them and reach out to help them all that you can.

However, we all know that workplace stress comes in all shapes and forms. And it's not just projects, tasks, and deadlines that can make you want to scream – the people you work with also play a major role in your frustration level as well as your ability to be productive. Not getting along with a co-worker means you have to face the stress of the situation day in and day out. There's no escaping the people you spend 40 hours or more a week with.

As one management writer puts it, as surely as some people bring out your best and your worst, you can be one of the people who brings out the best in people at their worst - understand where they're coming from and where you can help. You can't deal with and change things you don't first learn about and understand. And, you will be a much stronger and happier worker if you take the high road and seek to help those giving you grief. It's a good thing.

Fortunately, there are methods to dealing with the often agonizing situations. You'd be surprised how much you can do to change a difficult co-worker into a manageable, and perhaps even likeable, one. Don't waste time, or even come unglued on account of someone you can't stand. Instead, practice these following tips to make it through your work day in spite of a coworker who bugs the heck out of you.

"Complaining Employees Are Bad News"

Dear Dave,

Where I work, most of the employees bad mouth everything and everyone, person and it is driving me nuts. I am trying to stay positive, but it seems like my manager just looks the other way. Please print something that will get my manager to take notice and do something about this.

R

Dear R,

I have great empathy for managers. As a leader, one of the most difficult people to deal with is the expert complainer, the person on the team who is never happy, but does nothing about it, other than spread their miserable rants.

4

As one of my colleagues puts it, these folks rarely share the problem with anyone who has the authority to change it, and they rarely bring a solution to the table. Unfortunately your boss believes the best way to handle these people is to "do the Ostrich thing."

What Managers Can Do About Complaining Employees

Difficult employees constantly complain, mostly because it is a behavior that has worked for them in the past. They may not know any other behavior or they may choose this behavior when they think it will be most effective.

Here are some tips from management writer, Linda Swindling, who believes chronic complainers are often compared to school bullies, spoiled toddlers, whiny children, sneaky adolescents, and sullen teenagers. She says there are five categories of chronic complainers.

Whiners complain by showing disapproval, venting, or withdrawing. Whiners *appear* as martyrs, spoiled brats, and pouters.

Whiner Care and Feeding: Negotiate with whiners by listening and empathizing for a few minutes and then ask for concrete solutions. For example, "Wow, that has to be tough for you. How will you handle that?"

Complicators employ complaining tactics that frustrate, complicate, and create confusion. They *appear* as critics, nitpickers, know-it-alls, and micromanagers. They *want* to block change.

Complicator Care and Feeding: Negotiate with complicators by respecting the intellect of their rationale, thought processes, or designs. Present change as a logical addition and ask them to contribute.

Prima Donnas complain by seeking attention, gossiping, creating drama, and stirring up trouble. They *appear* brash, excessive, reactionary, and dramatic. They are comfortable in the spotlight, often seeking attention to the exclusion of others.

Prima Donna Care and Feeding: Negotiate with prima donnas by recognizing them, but avoid getting lost in their drama. Keep things simple with them and ask for simple responses about specific things from them.

Controllers use a variety of aggressive complaints in their attempts to reach an outcome, to control situations, and to control people. They *appear* to be tyrants, bullies, slave drivers, and bulldozers. They are aggressive, impatient, and intimidating.

Controller Care and Feeding: Negotiate with controllers by standing your ground. Be assertive and confident but not antagonistic. Let controllers know you are aware of problems and, if possible, let them decide the next direction.

Toxics are dangerous individuals who use complaints and misinformation to manipulate and poison the environment to further their self-absorbed agendas. They *appear* as narcissists and manipulators. They can adapt their behavior to please management, while tormenting coworkers and direct reports.

Toxic Care and Feeding: Negotiate with toxics by reminding yourself that you are a rational person and they are not. Acknowledge a toxic's comments to you and simply ask for the rationale behind their rants.

The reality is, positive people generate a far better work environment and are better contributors to a team and to the company. Your boss is there to help you solve problems, so work with your boss by letting him or her know that complainers are bringing good people down.

"Workplace Drama is Sickening"

Dear Dave,

I am a manager. The drama at my place of work is so thick you could cut it with a knife. People overreact and everything is a crisis. This leads to intense gossip and temper flair-ups. Things are out of hand. Advice?

P

Dear P,

When employees of differing personalities are put together, tempers will flare as they try to deal with one another. Most drama in the workplace is minor, but drama between employees that negatively affects everyone else in the workplace is another matter entirely.

Workplace drama is when employees over-act and over-react - this makes for a very tense environment. Heated misunderstandings happen even between mild-mannered people. No matter how great the hiring practices, we human beings create a lot of drama when we don't know how to see things clearly and react appropriately.

Why We Love Drama

I believe people - to varying degrees - enjoy drama. We have a constant desire to know what others are doing, how they're feeling, and mistakes they're making, and this desire exists, even while inside a professional environment.

The workplace can easily become an environment filled with temperamental people discussing and sharing sensitive, personal information, which creates a cesspool of social intrigue and suspense within the workplace. Working eight hours a day, five days a week is hard and throwing in a little emotion and drama throughout the week spices things up.

What to Do

First, diagnose the problem. Which of the four drama-driven personality types that management theorists Warner and Klemp describe are you dealing with? They are:

Complainers blame others and don't take responsibility for their actions.

Cynics are valued in the organization for their intellect, but only see the downside of a situation.

Controllers can't delegate and are master manipulators.

Caretakers are overly warm and fuzzy, and want everyone to like them.

Understanding who you are dealing with helps you decide your next course of action for drama reduction. Try these tips to address all 4 personalities:

Crucial conversation - After you've diagnosed the drama problem and determined the personality types you are dealing with, have a direct conversation with the offenders about their behavior. Explain what behavior is and is not acceptable.

Adapt to drama personalities - Each personality type requires a different management style - you've got to be able to choose different approaches. For example, it's often good to take a softer approach with complainers and caretakers, but still be direct and assertive.

8

Stop gossip - As soon as you hear drama-producing gossip spreading, put a stop to it. If you can narrow a rumor down to the biggest violators, counsel them individually and try to halt the spread of any misinformation.

Separate fact from fiction – You must manage by truth. When facing any interpersonal conflict, it is crucial to keep an open mind until you hear all points of view. Then rectify the situation with a meeting, if necessary, with all affected employees, so the truth can be heard.

Carefully confront - Most people, who thrive on drama, believe in their drama, and they think their behavior is valid. Be tactful, but firm, and establish the fact that you can no longer accept the drama.

One of the most effective ways to end drama in the workplace is to catch it early, before it gets out of hand. Therefore, try to be upfront with your employees about company news that is factual and impacts them directly, so reality can drive thinking and behavior.

"Ways to Get People to Open Up"

Dear Dave,

How can I get people to open up and be truthful at work? I am frustrated that my employees say everything is great at the company or with my management when we're face-to-face, but then the real opinions surface in quiet conversations amongst the employees.

R

Dear R,

I can remember clearly being frustrated by this issue myself as a manager - especially when I was the new "manager kid" on the block. I heard a lot of happy talk, but deep down the employees had a lot of baggage, opinions, and emotions.

At first I thought it was me and I must appear to be some unapproachable Neanderthal. I thought about all the reasons why someone might be uncomfortable speaking their mind to me, whether in a one-on-one meeting or in a group meeting:

They could be reserved quiet types

They don't want to appear dumb by not knowing all of the answers

They don't want to be seen as high- maintenance, needy employees

They may take more time to ponder things

They might think their ideas don't count, because no one has listened to them in the past

I guess the reason could be any or all of the above. The challenge was, how can I get my employees to feel comfortable with approaching me at any time with anything?

What I did

Feeling empathy for my team members, and understanding that they weren't all as comfortable speaking out as I was, led me to try some different things:

Get people to open up – No one wants to look like the bad guy, or be considered a negative trouble-maker, so your employees have a natural tendency to not say what they believe. Try asking, "Are there things we or you are doing that just do not make sense and are a waste of time? Meshed with your open-door policy, this gives people a comfort level to say something they might not otherwise say.

Practice active listening - I made sure I gave my employees my full attention. It is crucial that you appear present and alert for what your employees have to say. I would truly listen, ask probing questions, never interrupt, and frequently paraphrase back to them to confirm understanding.

Don't be overly judgmental – First, always thank your employees for what they shared, unless what they shared was going to have an immediate negative impact on the business, the culture, or the productivity, I would step back, take a breath, and not give an immediate opinion. This shows you are not shooting the messenger and are doing your best to calmly digest the statements.

Send out an agenda of discussion items – Meetings are mandatory and some companies handle them well and some don't evolve any intellectual thinking or knowledge sharing whatsoever. I would share topics and agenda items ahead of time. If you want ideas and feedback, you can't expect people to come into the meeting stone cold and not know what the discussion items are, or even the general purpose of the meeting.

After-Action feedback – After a project or plan has been launched or concluded, I always asked for feedback regarding what went well and what definitely needs improvement. This is a real-time or post-mortem autopsy to discover and discuss those nagging things that upset the plan and were totally ignored or disregarded. It is important to discuss the well-functioning aspects, too, so these things can be capitalized on in the future.

It took some time for me to be consistent in these behaviors and for people to begin to embrace face-to-face honest communication, but, ultimately, it led to open and honest dialogue and increased trust and collaboration.

"Dealing With Negativity"

Dear Dave,

My coworkers are always complaining. It doesn't matter what is happening, the first thing they do is become extremely negative and find things wrong. I think the thing that sets them off most is when our manager asks for a change of some kind. They're not happy with the ways things are and they are not happy when changes are proposed. How can I cope?

M

Dear M,

I know exactly what you mean. I worked with people who could depress a clown convention. Instead of finding what may be right about something, they would instantly launch into tirades about why something was wrong.

Your workplace coworkers have created for themselves a self-perpetuating and self-reinforcing system of negativity. Worse, they devour opportunities to drag others – like you – into their web of poisoned mindsets. This makes for a systemic problem that management must address.

On the other hand, sometimes normally positive people are negative. Some of the time, too, their reasons for negativity are legitimate. But, like any workplace challenge, it's not what happens as much as how you react to it.

Misery Loves Company

First, let me state my definition of a 'Nega-toxic' person - A person who complains and dumps their problems on you but doesn't do anything to change their situation. Someone who is not supportive, makes you feel badly about yourself, and shoots down your ideas and decisions.

Nega-toxic people are usually in a place in their life where they are not open to constructive feedback or changing, so they are stuck in their current situation and don't have the insight to see beyond their own struggles.

Psychologists say there is a general tendency for everyone to remember negative things more strongly and in more detail than positive experiences. However, workplace negativity becomes a huge problem when all that is remembered is negative, or any new thing is viewed as negative.

Negative people can find something wrong in any situation. They are expert complainers, cynics, worriers, and victims. Unfortunately, negative people may not be concerned with the devastating effect their behavior has on others; they simply want to get rid of their own uncomfortable feelings in the fastest way possible.

How to Cope

I suggest you deal with genuinely negative people by spending as little time with them as possible. If you are forced, through your role in the company, to work with a negative person, set limits. Do not allow yourself to be drawn into negative discussions. Tell the negative coworker, you prefer to think about your job in realistic, but positive terms.

Kill them with kindness - if a negative coworker is peddling their ware, try to be as nice to them as possible. You can't change anyone, but your positive energy and outlook on the situation will make it less likely for your coworkers to continue with their negative behavior towards you. Lead by example, and be a positive source of positive energy at your office.

Set boundaries and standards and do not lower your standards to connect with negative people. Even in the face of an argument, do not lose your head and sink down into the negativity that surrounds you.

If all else fails, talk to your own manager, or human resources staff, about the challenges you are experiencing in dealing with the negative person. If the negativity persists or grows, and affects your ability to professionally perform your work, you may want to consider moving on.

"When Coworkers Claim All of the Credit"

Dear Dave,

I'm not a "glory hog," but I work hard and believe I should be recognized for my accomplishments. My coworkers are only worried about getting praised no matter who did the work. It is sickening to watch this. What can I do?

S

Dear S,

People who do the work should be given credit for their accomplishments. It is a manager's responsibility to evaluate what work was done, who did it, and how effectively it was done. Then, due credit should be rewarded to the individuals and teams that dug in and made things happen.

It is only right that, when you've put long hours into a project, or task, you want proper credit for it. It can be frustrating to watch a co-worker(s) present your collective team work as his or her own. When someone hogs the limelight, you feel violated and robbed to some extent.

Why some are "glory hogs"

I believe why, some people – both coworkers and even managers - want to be a "glutton for glory" and claim they were *most* responsible for things getting done is, they know in their hearts and minds they probably did "diddly squat" (I like that term).

So, we are talking here about slackers again – who really know they are slackers – but, know they cannot let their "slackiness" show. They overcompensate by totally denying reality and go so far as actually claiming they are responsible – if not totally responsible – for any and all achievements.

My theory is, the best, hardest-working people are typically not glory pigs and just get busy doing things that must get done. They know they are doing good work and they also know that others are claiming that work was their own. However, the hard-working people are usually really nice people, too, and they let it go … thinking management may finally wise up to realize who is really doing what.

I think this "con game" only goes on so long and the true achievers rise to the surface, while the "slackers" are finally recognized as people contributing little. I call this "workplace Karma" and the good get the good and the bad get the bad.

How to handle

Even though it's agonizing to hear people whine about how busy they are, your best bet is to make sure you keep just keep working and devote your time and energy to the things you have to get done instead. Here are some other tips:

Confront the "glory hogs" - Have a calm, candid, face-to-face conversation with the coworker(s). Give specific examples that identify the fact that both of you – or the whole team – collectively completed a project or task. Often, just identifying the behavior will put an end to it.

Talk to your manager - If you can't resolve the issue with your coworker, go to your manager. Remain calm and avoid whining, or finger pointing. In addition, come to the meeting with evidence that demonstrates work was done in a collective manner.

Early intervention - The next time you work on a project with the offenders, be clear up front about roles, responsibilities, and accountabilities. Also, agree that you'll collectively share the visibility and appreciation for your efforts.

I can personally attest to the fact that it's not fun having to deal with credit stealing co-workers, but it's crucial that you stay professional and keep working hard, and not play the "glory hog game."

"New Employees Face Challenges"

Dear Dave,

At my company, some people have retired or have left, mostly because of layoffs. Some jobs have been filled by new employees and, in many cases, existing employees have just absorbed the extra work. The problem is that, the new employees are treated very unkindly by my coworkers. There is almost resentment that these new people have work when others have been let go. I am trying to be friendly and helpful to these new people. How can I help them?

P

Dear P,

Obviously, your heart is in the right place and I applaud your willingness to help these folks get acclimated in a challenging environment where, yes, existing employees will feel resentment that friends may have been let go and these new people now have their jobs.

It is tough enough learning a new job, let alone trying to 'fit in' and adjust to the mood and tone of the work culture, and mistrust sensed by veteran workers. It is human nature to protect what you have and your coworkers have been beaten up to some extent, and new workers pose a threat to the well-being and "way things were' that your coworkers enjoyed.

Acclimation Is Not Automatic

One new study surveyed 464 employees and asked, "What is the greatest challenge for workers starting at a new company?" Here's what the workers said:

Getting used to new culture and co-workers (37%)

Learning new policies and processes (23%)

Adapting to a new routine (22%)

Building personal confidence (10%), and

Other/don't know (8%).

Frankly, I never will understand how respondents 'don't' know' – they must sense something. I digress.

These study findings reveal that, new employees have the roughest time adapting to that predominant, ever-present, and often daunting force ... the work culture. The culture is created by the people – both staff and management - and, in your case, the culture is one that makes new employees appear about as welcome as a telemarketer at supper time.

How to Help New Hires

Even though you may not be their manager, there are many things both you can do to help these new folks get acclimated. Remember, you were new once, so reflect back on how you felt and how others treated you ... good or bad.

Encourage the new people to continue to learn as much about the organization as possible, both through conversations with you and others. Spend time discussing the organization's current strategy and the related goals and challenges.

It is best to try to inform the new employees about 'what really goes on' at work and provide them some idea about the culture and who the power mongers are. Also, tell the new hires they should spend a great deal of time upfront observing and listening, so as not to make bad first impressions by assuming too much, or appearing as all-knowing.

Make sure to introduce the new hire to the "right people' as soon as possible. Employees need to know what to expect, and will benefit from getting a sense of his/her new team's responsibilities, style, concerns, etc. to help prepare for the first few weeks.

If possible, become an unofficial mentor - someone to whom the new hire can go to for objective advice and questions. Try to help the new people understand the institutional history, the leadership team, and the organization's strengths and weaknesses.

It's hard to be the new kid in class. Helping new people understand the culture of the organization goes along way for helping them adjust smoothly.

"Are Teams Overrated?"

Quote of the Week: "As a coach, I play not my eleven best, but my best eleven."

– Knute Rockne, Notre Dame Football Coach

Dear Dave,

I think teams are overrated. Most teams I have been on have always ended up being less productive than they should be. Also, it seems that one or two people end up doing all of the work, while everyone else just preaches and complains. I might as well just work on my own – I get more done. I know you are going to tell me about the wonders of teams, but I just don't see it.

P

Dear P,

Listen, you are preaching to the choir. I, too, have been on teams that did not work together, did very little, and could not make decisions. These teams were "masters of meetings" and believed they were effective and productive, simply because they were able to schedule another meeting.

However, the team approach is widely accepted by organizations – including Mayo Clinic – for using multiple perspectives, inputs, and talents to produce something better than what a group of independent thinkers could put together on their own.

Don't get me wrong: I believe in the value and power of the individual thinker, but, what we enjoy today in our every-day lives, are the results of people thinking and working together to hit aggressive targets.

Why Teams are Dysfunctional

As you know, I teach management courses. Often when we come to the topic of teams in my classes, I can see my students' eyes glaze over with a look of … "alright, let's just get through this, because I know we need to cover teams."

I throw out terms like synergy (the work of two people working together produces more than two people working independently), innovation, effectiveness, and collaborative problem-solving … all created and produced by teams. Then, I give them a team project activity and sometimes see one or two people playing with their phones.

It is at that point, I tell the class – without singling out any individuals - that this is a team assignment and I ask and expect that everyone thinks and contributes. This often helps, but I feel like I just became some autocratic thug, who had to pounce on those team members, who were less than enthused about the activity.

Granted, some team members will throw themselves on the team assignment with a vigor that may leave some people feeling lost in the dust. These well-intentioned team assignment "pouncers" mean well, but they must become better at drawing out the thinking and contributions of others.

Then, we also have team problems, such as unclear goals, limited resources, lack of analysis and planning, no sensed purpose and urgency, and a plethora of other team problems that good managers could correct and keep from happening from the onset of the team mission.

The concept of "leaderless teams" is nonsense – in my opinion - because leaders always emerge in teams. It is when these "emerging leaders' control everything, ride people like rented mules, and believe the only good thinking is their thinking is when the real problems start to happen. Good emerging team leaders clarify the challenges, delegate work, and motivate people to get it done.

I ask that you not give up on teams and take a look at how your future teams can learn, prosper, and contribute together. Also, it is best if the team is composed of people with different skills, backgrounds, experiences, and views.

Finally, teams work better and produce greater results when debate (respectful) occurs and people challenge each other. Agreeing just to agree – for efficiency sake – is not effectiveness.

"Accountability is a Responsibility"

Dear Dave,

A problem at my company has gotten out of hand. I think most, not all, employees are just not accountable for their work and what is expected of them. Many of my fellow employees have become experts at passing the buck and having brilliant excuses for not doing or completing things. Can this situation be turned around?

B

Dear B,

This is a management problem, because one of the most important tasks for management is establishing clear accountability. Accordingly, managers must focus their energy on hiring the "right and best people," defining jobs, roles, and goals, and then figure out who to reward or reprimand.

The goal is to motivate responsible people to do their jobs and the assumption is that, people will perform more effectively if they know exactly what they are supposed to accomplish and what will happen, or how they will be rewarded, if they make or miss the target.

Things go wrong

Way too often, accountability becomes weak and confusing: Rewards are misapplied, or not provided, consequences are watered down or never occur, and people do not see the direct connection between their job expectations, results, and recognition.

I think the worst thing that can happen is when people - who underperform, or do not perform at all – get rewarded, and rewarded just as much as those that have busted their tail (official business phrase). When this happens, even the greatest performers will say, "I'm done. Why am I working so hard and getting the same recognition/rewards as the slackers?"

My management colleagues believe there are three common reasons why organizations become accountability anemic: the complexity, numerous levels, and multiple departments of an organization's structure; the fact that work processes and systems are constantly changing; and, maybe the most significant reason for poor accountability is that, "some" people work hard to avoid it.

I think it is becomingly increasingly difficult for individuals and teams to know whether their actions have impact, or how changes in one part of the workflow will impact others. As a result, it's easy for employees and teams to say that they did their jobs well, and any problems must have been caused by someone or somewhere else.

Responsible accountability

For managers, accountability is mandatory and it's not impossible to implement. Managers must help their employees and teams prioritize their responsibilities in relation to the company's goals. I would get employees involved – this will allow employees to feel more engaged and buy-into accountability demands. Managers can also do the following:

Uncover the reasons for unclear accountability – Have an accountability reasons, factors, and gaps discussion with your team and your fellow managers. Identify any negative systemic or cultural influences within your organization and devise ways to overcome them. Also, investigate whether or not employees have the skills and resources they need.

Clearly explain who is accountable for what and how results will be measured - Make sure you set clear expectations and define roles, goals, and deliverables before starting any project or task. At the same time, communicate the means of measuring productivity – so no one will need to guess how they will be assessed.

Reward performers and provide consequences for nonperformers – Ensure that those employees who understand their roles and expectations and deliver targeted results are rewarded and recognized. In the same vein, discipline those who repeatedly show a lack of responsibility.

Making accountability happen isn't always easy. However, clearly understood and effectively managed accountability of people and their roles are essential for productivity.

"Pay Attention to Workplace Tension"

Dear Dave,

Where I work, conflict and tension is all around me. People seem to antagonize each other and arguments are quite common. Why is there so much tension at work and what can be done about it? Management seems to just look the other way.

P

Dear P,

Yes, conflict occurs in every office to varying degrees and with almost every employee. While you can try and avoid conflict (good idea), you cannot escape conflict.

Conflict rarely resolves itself. In fact, conflict normally escalates if not dealt with proactively and properly. We all have seen what might have been a small tiff turn into a monumental problem if not resolved early on.

Every workplace is plagued with manipulative people who use emotion to create conflict in order to cover-up for their lack of substance. I won't even get into the personality types who thrive on conflict, but, trust me, there are many who try to make themselves feel better by making the lives of others quite difficult.

Good leaders recognize that developing effective conflict resolution skills are an essential component for building a sustainable, collaborative work environment. Unresolved conflict often results in loss of productivity, the stifling of creativity, and the creation of barriers to cooperation and collaboration.

What is conflict?

When I ask my MBA students to define workplace conflict, the responses range from the presence of negative situations to people having an extreme dislike for other people. Some define it as anger, distrust, or antagonism.

I believe that conflict does not need to be seen as just negative. In fact, it can be neutral or even positive. Conflict can simply be defined as creative tension and can actually be harnessed to challenge and change things.

However, left unaddressed, everyone, including the organization, suffers. Good people leave. Customers notice and leave. And, there is just a general presence of cynicism present that makes everyone uneasy ... and confrontational.

Handling Conflict

While having a conflict resolution structure is important, it is dependent upon the ability of all employees to understand the benefits of conflict resolution. The following tips will help to more effectively handle conflicts in the workplace:

Figure out why everyone's upset - You want to bring all of the issues out in to the open. In order to resolve a workplace conflict you have to understand what the real problem is. Assess the impact of the problems you're faced with, along with the consequences.

Deal with it - By proactively seeking out areas of potential conflict, and appropriately intervening in a just and decisive fashion, you will likely prevent certain conflicts from ever arising.

Pick your battles - Ask yourself how important this problem really is. Does it really affect you or is it something that has nothing to do with you? Is it an ongoing problem or a one-time incident?

Listen to all sides - Make sure that along with any emotional information, you discuss specific facts or events that led up to or inflamed the situation. Surface the issues and remain objective.

Remain professional and calm. Disputes are going to happen, but try to remain calm and unemotional. Remember that two wrongs do not make a right.

The reality is that the root of most conflict is either born out of poor communication, or the inability to control one's emotions. Accordingly, people must communicate effectively and stay in control of their emotions.

"Helping a Coworker Build Confidence"

Dear Dave,

I have a coworker who is bright and works hard. She is a very likeable and helpful person. However, her self-confidence is terrible and I know this is holding her back. I feel bad for her and would like to help her. How can I help her be more confident in herself?

T

Dear T,

First, let me say that I think you are a kind, generous person for caring about this coworker – this shows that you are a leader as well as someone who 'gets it'.

Your coworker is suffering from self-esteem issues, which is something that is far too common in individuals at work and in other aspects of one's life. How you feel about yourself –

your self-confidence, ego, and sense of self-worth - affects how we communicate, perform, and relate to others.

For whatever reason(s), your friend is effective, but has developed a pattern of thinking, where she believes she does not measure up to others, or to what others may expect of her. The opposite is individuals who have a great deal of sense self-confidence and may not even be effective at all.

Confidence 'Coaching' is Systemic

The capacity to build and maintain self-esteem in oneself and in others is one of the key competencies for leadership. When we help our fellow employees improve their performance, teach others new skills, mentor other employees to realize their potential, or build or maintain self-esteem in others, we will help foster a productive and fulfilling workplace.

One Successful business person I know once told me that, the key to business is that you become successful by making all around you successful. As your friend rises - through your help and guidance - you will also rise.

This goes on to mean that, your confidence in her will help build her confidence in herself, which she will return to you making you sense greater confidence – it becomes a reinforcing system of well-being and positive thinking.

Now, don't get me wrong; I don't believe we should go around building the confidence of those who are purposefully destructive and willingly negative – that would be like throwing gas on a forest fire. However, as we rove around during our day (and work day), there are obvious opportunities for us to help good, hard-working people suffering from self-esteem issues.

We Are How We Feel

I will state upfront that I am not a board-certified psychologist, but I am an observer and participant in life. Plus, I have a great deal of empathy for others and the struggles they go through. Accordingly, I am sensitive to what others are going through and how they feel about themselves … as obviously, you are, too.

Today, organizations want a workforce with a higher level of interdependence, self-reliance, self-trust, and the capacity to exercise initiative. This means that organizations need large numbers of people with confidence and self-esteem.

We are all leaders, whether we like it or not, and, as a leader, you are, whether you know it or not, a role model. The higher your self-esteem, the more likely it is you'll be able inspire the best in others.

In that vein, if your coworker does superior work, or makes an excellent decision, invite her to explore how and why it happened. Do not limit yourself simply to praise. By asking appropriate questions, help raise her consciousness about what made the achievement possible, thereby increasing the likelihood that others like it will occur in the future.

"Rudeness at Work Hurts"

Dear Dave,

A few of the people I work with are just plain rude to each other. This is getting me down and I know some of my coworkers have been hurt many times. Why would they behave this way? What should managers do about this behavior?

M

Dear M,

Rude and disrespectful coworkers exist at virtually every workplace and communicating with them – mostly, because you have to – is slightly less painful than a root canal. They're rude, because of something that's going on with them. Don't take their behavior personally.

The more subtle and malicious forms of rudeness include gossiping, backstabbing, spreading rumors, and sabotaging others' work. In one large study, a staggering 98% employees reported experiencing rude behavior at work.

Some HR experts call rude behavior, "incivility." I say rude is rude and it is what it is. Accordingly, it must be dealt with quickly and effectively. If the behavior is left untreated, the door is wide open for the rude offenders and others to think it is OK to act this way. Wrong!

The Effects of Rudeness

Simply, if an employee is rude to colleagues or customers, it can damage your firm's reputation and poison the culture and morale. Ultimately, this can lead to a loss of sales, or a fall in productivity. It is not uncommon for good people to quit their jobs, because of a rude environment.

My management colleagues tell me rudeness hurts the feelings of staff, stifles communication, and hampers innovation, and you can imagine what new employees think when they are thrown into a rude environment – they are thinking, "Get me out of here."

Customers notice. Suppliers notice. Everyone sees it. Think about any time you were in a store or another work setting, and workers were being rude to each other. When I was in such a setting, I not only felt extremely uncomfortable, but I also believed that management was not doing their job.

I cannot elaborate on all of the reasons people are just plain rude. However, rude people are unhappy people and they like making others unhappy, because "misery loves company." Rude people hate well-adjusted, nice, happy people – they are a threat to their being.

Managers Must Act

Managers must assess the rude environment and talk to the rude offenders. In their discussion with the "attack pack," managers must be specific about what behaviors are happening and what negative impact they have on others, and the company as a whole.

However, if informal action fails, management may need to initiate some form of disciplinary action, especially if you or another employee makes a formal complaint about a particular coworker.

In extreme cases of rude behavior, managers may need to take action for instant dismissal, because of gross misconduct. It is undesirable to allow things to reach this point and, if it did, I question whether the manager should be retained.

Coping With Rudeness

Be assertive. If a co-worker is rude, it's important to stand up to the person. Acknowledge the problem in an assertive manner without insulting your co-worker, and deal with it as soon as possible.

If the problems persist, go to a HR representative or a manager. Be truthful and prepare a strong case with documentation, and share it without getting too negative or defensive.

Finally, understand that you cannot control others. Letting the situation go, and realizing that the problem is the coworker's and not yours, is best. The only thing you can control is your reaction to another's behavior.

"Camaraderie at Work Can Be a Competitive Advantage"

Dear Dave,

What are your thoughts on employees being best friends at work? Doesn't this possibly create situations where people will goof off more and then take their mind off of their job?

I am all for employees being friendly, but being too friendly may create a party environment.

R

Dear R,

Not surprisingly, workers enjoy their jobs more when they have friendships with colleagues. But camaraderie is more than just having fun; it's also about creating a common sense of purpose and identity.

Companies should create and value camaraderie as a competitive advantage for recruiting top talent, retaining employees, and improving engagement, creativity, and productivity. Many companies engage in corporate activities such as wellness competitions, community service events, and other activities to build a sense of teamwork and togetherness.

Survey after survey shows that employee engagement at work is at an all-time low. One way to help improve engagement at work is to foster friendships. Staff with strong bonds - teams that know and care about each other beyond what's required of their tasks and roles - can create a collaborative and collegial culture that gets things done.

Research also shows that workers are happier in their jobs when they have friendships with coworkers. Employees report that when they have friends at work, their job is more fun, enjoyable, worthwhile, and satisfying. Gallup found that close work friendships boost employee satisfaction by 50% and people with a best friend at work are seven times more likely to engage fully in their work.

More friendly benefits

Camaraderie goes beyond just having fun. It is also about creating a common sense of purpose and the mindset that we have a mission and shared destiny. In short, camaraderie promotes a group loyalty that results in a shared commitment to and discipline toward even difficult work. The opposite would be employees coming to work, acting like lifeless robots, and talking to each other only if they need to borrow a stapler.

Friends at work also form a strong social support network for each other, both personally and professionally. Whether congratulating people for job advancements, consoling each other in times of personal need, or lending needed advice, comradeship at work can boost an employee's spirit and provide needed emotional assistance.

Innovative companies - among them Google and Southwest Airlines - have built strong reputations for fostering comradeship at work. These companies have found that a culture nurturing friendships offer a competitive advantage for recruiting top employees, retaining employees, and improving engagement, creativity, and productivity. Good people are attracted to companies that are "friend friendly."

As a leader, you can foster a culture of camaraderie by being clear about what you want the culture to be within your organization. Mingle with employees and show that work is challenging, but can be engaging. Leverage your employees' talents by encouraging their ideas and help your people must feel proud of the products and services your organization provides. How you relate to your people will determine how they relate to each other.

To be honest, there are some negative aspects for you to mind, including: professional jealousy, groupthink, negative cliques, loss of work time to socializing, and broken friendships. However, these are all manageable and the benefits of positive relationships far outweigh any negative outcomes.

In summary, people in organizations need to work together. So, managers and employees need to foster collaboration, trust, personal relationships, fun, and support. In an increasingly global and virtual environment, challenges for employees and managers will be to cultivate these personal relationships and build collaboration and unity.

"Employees Must Earn Their Positions"

Dear Dave,

Our company is experiencing some economic challenges, which is causing a great deal of fear among employees. I believe my company is currently assessing all employees and the work they do to determine which jobs are critical and which employees should stay. The problem is that most of the employees feel they are entitled to keep their job simply because the company *owes* them employment. I believe the best workers should remain employed, not those who "slide by." I also believe there are many jobs that should be reviewed to determine if they are even needed. The stress and frustration levels are high.

M

Dear M,

I agree with you. I think tough times call for tough measures. For several years now – like never before – all companies are looking at the worth of jobs and the contributions of the employees to determine what and who adds true value and effectiveness.

My greatest concern is when companies only use tenure (years of service) or favoritism when making choices about keeping people. I will get hate mail for this, but I think you need to be a dedicated, effective worker and earn your job every day, and those who do should be kept on the payroll, and those who don't should go.

No Free Lunch

Unless you are a contracted worker, all employees are 'at will' employees, meaning, they can leave when they want to and that companies can dismiss them when they want. Employment at will means that an employee can be terminated at any time without any reason. It also means that an employee can quit without reason.

Entitlement means people (workers) believe that they are worthy of a certain level of respect and rewards, and they are determined to get that level of respect and reward, no matter what. As my Dad always said, "It's not what you say, it's what you do that counts." In short, you need to prove your worth every day and all day.

Accordingly, no one owes anyone anything. Neither the company nor the employee should sense a superiority or deservingness of any kind (entitlement) when considering the work to be done, who should be doing it, and how long the employment relationship lasts.

Companies want productivity, profits, and survival. Workers want pay, long-term employment, and meaningful jobs. However, the wants of companies may – in reality - mean they have to make strategically critical decisions about jobs and people that may displace even effective workers.

Breaking the Entitlement Cycle

Organizations want less 'entitled' employees – those who believe they will always have a job until retirement regardless of what they produce, or those who believe the company owes them an annual raise or a promotion because of seniority, not demonstrated competence.

Organizations must hire more 'accountable' employees – those who believe that their position is only justified as long as they contribute something of value and they are responsible for developing better ways to serve the customer and the company.

One manager I know thinks our culture seems to be a breeding ground for entitlement thinking. If a culture of non-accountability pervades within an organization, the manager has a tough challenge, because entitlement will stifle continuous improvement. This is both a hiring problem and a management problem.

Managers: If you want empowerment, accountability, responsibility, then be empowered, accountable, and responsible yourself. Your actions will speak louder than your words. People define you by your actions, so lead by example. Then, insist on the same from your workers.

"The Biggest Mistake is Letting Mistakes Slip By"

Dear Dave,

I work for a large company. A lot of good people who work here and they work hard. Plus, they show a great deal of pride and integrity in their work. However, I have a couple of coworkers who make a lot of mistakes and worse, they try to cover their mistakes up without doing anything to correct them. They seem to get away with these errors. I am not their manager, just a fellow employee.

H,

Dear H,

I always ask my MBA students: Success is easy to deal with, but how well do you handle your mistakes? Do you embrace them as opportunities to showcase your leadership skills, or do you shy away and look to cover up your flaws?

The key to overcoming the tendency to cover up our flaws and mistakes is to understand that doing so is a failure that typically makes the problem worse. Also, our inability to own up actually decreases our personal credibility and trust with others, contrary to the belief of many political and business leaders.

Making errors at work can be embarrassing and many people become defensive or evasive when faced with a mistake that they made. However, the best way to handle a mistake is to own up to it, fix it, and be sure to learn from the mistake.

Also, it could be worse: These people could be pointing the finger at you or others as being the ones who made the mistakes. There are no limits what people will do to prevent themselves from looking bad.

'Coming Clean' is Leadership

Coming clean and admitting errors takes courage: a characteristic of quality leadership. Admitting your errors also invites others to do the same, which contributes to the creation of a healthy work environment.

You can help foster this authenticity, even when the mistake is not your own. When others make errors, forgive them for the things they've done, and do not criticize them. Separate the person from the mistake and give them a chance to make amends. Let them 'save face'.

The best leaders understand that it's how they handle their biggest mistakes that truly define them. The next time you, yourself, are the cause of a workplace screw-up, do not shy away from it. Put aside your ego, admit your mistake, apologize, and follow through with action to fix it.

The ability to admit that you've made a mistake shows not only character, but also confidence, because you're not afraid of how you'll look. In contrast, making excuses comes across as shallow and immature.

Fixing the Problem

I think it is human nature to want to cower and hide rather than confess to mistakes that have taken place at work for fear of being reprimanded, given a written warning, or out of fear of being fired. These are natural feelings, but for those who lie when the mistakes are uncovered, will risk losing their job anyway.

However, I would go to your manager and explain what you see. You may not win any popularity contests, but it is the right thing to do. Use a calm, straightforward style with no blame or accusations.

Tell your boss your purpose in coming to him or her is to help create an environment in which quality can thrive. Your concern is that covering up mistakes sends the wrong signal and is bad for business.

"No Room for the Blame Game"

Dear Dave,

My problem is that all of the employees and managers are experts at blaming others for mistakes that happen. Everyone makes mistakes and no one is perfect. I think it makes more sense to correct problems than to worry about who to point the finger at. What do you think?

T

Dear T,

Blaming is a way of simply not wanting to be accountable for something that has happened. Blame carries with it a lot of negative connotation for many people, including yours truly, and so it is frequently something that people do not want to have associated with themselves.

A competitive approach to any difficulty occurs where people deny that their actions may have influenced a situation and 'point the finger' at others. Where it is clear their actions did contribute to a difficulty they tend to say they were 'forced' in some way to do it by others.

Whatever the error, pointing the finger at someone else or something else might seem trivial, but, in organizations where blame is all too common, employees are likely to be less creative and perform poorly.

The Blame Game or "It Ain't Me, Babe!"

Playing the blame game never works. Research shows that people who blame others for their mistakes lose status, learn less, and perform worse relative to those who own up to their mistakes. I agree with the research.

Groups and organizations with a fierce culture of blame have a serious disadvantage when it comes to learning, innovation, and productive risk-taking. In short, nobody wants to stick their neck out, because they may become responsible for any errors that might occur.

That's why creating a culture of psychological safety is one of the most important things a leader can do. But this isn't easy, and some recent findings offer another reason why: blaming is contagious.

When a problem occurs and the blame approach is used, there is an unwillingness by those involved to question 'why' things happened. It is much easier to just single out an individual and say, "There's the culprit - it wasn't me." Sadly, this is playground behavior.

I think the tight economy is causing the virus of blame to fester. People do not want to look bad when problems occur, so it is easier to find a scapegoat. It is more than ego protection; it is viewed by 'blamers' as critical for survival. The truth is, those who 'fess up' will be looked upon more favorably.

Admit It! Deal with It! Learn From It! Move On!

To do your part in helping to create a culture of error ownership, try this approach:

1) Acknowledge that mistakes or misunderstandings will always happen and see them as learning opportunities

2) Focus on what the details of the mistake or misunderstanding were in order to gain more clarity, again with a view to them being a learning opportunity

3) Place a priority on finding out 'What happened?' or 'How did it happen?' rather than 'Who did it?'

4) Set an example by confidently taking ownership for failures.

5) Always focus on learning. Creating a culture where learning — rather than avoiding mistakes — is the top priority will help to ensure that people feel free talk about and learn from their errors.

Knowing we can accept responsibility when things go wrong means we can also accept credit when things go well. There is absolutely no shame in being able to admit to yourself, or others, that you made mistakes.

"Slackers Are Dead Weight"

Dear Dave,

Yesterday, I had to stay late and finish a project, because another member of my team took off without completing his share of the work. Other people on our team have also picked up the slack for this same person on many occasions, so it's

not just me, but I'm really starting to feel like I am being used. I am sick and tired of working with slackers.

R

Dear R,

You are not alone and "slackers" are all too common in the modern workplace. Research finds that slackers not only drop the ball – or never really picked it up – but, they can reduce team enthusiasm, momentum, and performance.

One manager I know says, without realizing it, a highly motivated team can fall into a state of complacency when slackers can adversely impact a group's performance.

Slacker by My Definition

A slacker is someone who doesn't really care about the work at hand and does as little as possible to get by. A slacker misses deadlines and often responds negatively to motivation.

Sadly, it's systemic, and other group members take on the same characteristics, further driving the team into complacency. Others may respond by withdrawing, or trying their best to ignore the slacker. Just realize most group members undergo some level of stress and frustration.

Slackers are clever - they are the ones that compliment you (ingratiation), then ask you to do something for them in the same breath. They always have excuses about why they can't attend meetings, or fulfill their responsibilities – often very creative ones.

The effort that each group member exerts to deal with slacker is wasted energy that could be applied to the critical tasks at hand. Also, the team's momentum and progress suffer when a slacker's work must be picked up..

Attack the Slacker

I know it's hard to cope with slackers, but there are things you can do. The first thing is to try and stay calm and don't let the slacker's neglect get to you. I also think it is best to confront him and explain that he should really change his behavior. Here are more tips:

Stay focused on your work – Don't fall victim to the "slackiness." Any slacking on your part diminishes your credibility when it comes time to address this slacker's laziness, as he can simply turn around and point the finger at you.

Say no - If you make a habit out of doing others' work, then it could backfire. For example, this slackers may think, "If she's going to just finish the job for me, then why should I try?" You have a job to do yourself and that comes first.

Sell the benefits of all members doing their parts - Communicate that work completion stress could be avoided and morale could improve if all members pull their own weight. Sell the fact that teams thrive on everyone doing their part.

Confront the behavior - Sometimes all a slacker needs is for someone to call attention to the behavior. Share your concerns and be specific about the behavior that troubles you without being threatening or negative.

Finally, if you feel you're being taken advantage of on a regular basis and that you have confronted the behavior, but none of your efforts to resist are working, you may feel it's time to speak to your manager about the situation.

Chapter 2 – Lots More Management Stuff

Management is less about the needs of the manager, and more about the needs of the people and the organization he or she are leading. Management styles are not something to be tried on like different pairs of shoes, to see which fits. Rather, they should be adapted to the particular demands of the situation, the people, and the level of difficulty and tension present. These are the analytical requirements of the people involved and the particular challenges facing the organization.

By definition, management in all business and organizational activities is the act of coordinating the efforts of people to accomplish desired goals and objectives using available resources efficiently and effectively. Text books tell us management comprises planning, organizing, staffing, leading or directing, and controlling an organization (a group of one or more people or entities) or effort for the purpose of accomplishing a goal. That's a mouthful, but managers wear a lot of hats.

Since all organizations can be viewed as interconnected systems of people, parts, and processes, management can also be defined as the momentum of human action, including design, to facilitate the production of useful outcomes from a system. This means that all managers have the opportunity to manage and develop oneself, a prerequisite to attempting to manage and develop others.

Managers have to perform many roles in an organization and how they handle various situations will depend on their style of management. A management style is an overall method of leadership used by a manager.

I believe there are two sharply contrasting management styles: Autocratic and Permissive: The Autocratic: Leader makes all decisions and does not seek the inputs, ideas, and feedback of the employees. The Permissive Leader permits and invites employees to take part in decision making and also gives them a considerable degree of autonomy in completing routine work activities - empowerment. But, it is safe to say that, managers must also adjust their styles according to the situation and the people that they are presented with and determine which style is best.

The problems that arise stem from the fact that the manager is dealing with people, and they have thoughts, emotions, feelings, and beliefs. Accordingly, this makes for an interesting arrangement, because the manager may be thinking one thing and the employee(s) is thinking something else. This creates clashes. Read on to see how my letter responses may benefit you, or at least help you formulate more questions about management in the workplace.

"Managing Someone You Don't Like"

Dear Dave,

I manage several people and I get along well with almost all of them. However, there is one employee I have tried my hardest to like and warm up to – and it just is not there. I think he and I have personality conflicts and I can't help but treat him differently from everyone else. What can I do?

T

Dear T,

I believe we can't like everyone, but if we manage people, we need to get over it. Not everyone will win your popularity contest.

However, if these "unlikable" people are causing trouble and not doing their job, they do not deserve to be liked … nor employed. As a manager, it is crucial to recognize the difference between an employee who is underperforming and one who is just unlikable.

Managers tend to be closer to employees who are like them, act nice, don't make waves, flatter them, and don't deliver bad news. But, it's often those who provoke or challenge you - the people you find hard to like – who may provide fresh insights for innovation.

I know it's not possible to build a team comprised entirely of people you'd invite to Sunday dinner, but disliking this employee can cause problems. Consciously or unconsciously, you might mismanage him, or treat him unfairly, and fail to see the real benefits he can provide.

See things differently

First, stop seeing your relationships with colleagues in terms of who you like and who you don't like. Your job as a manager isn't necessarily to be friends with the people who work for you – however, it is your job to be friendly.

Your responsibility is to come across as professional, supportive, and positive. That means that you need to focus on his work and professional development. However, if his behaviors are negatively impacting his effectiveness, or the wellbeing of teammates, then it's time for a crucial conversation.

But again, you should be approaching him without emotion - it's about objectively viewing performance and behaviors. Do some reflection and analyze the situation. Ask yourself: Is he creating bad working relationships with others? Is he openly challenging your authority? Is he creating negativity in the working environment?

The answers to these questions will help you determine if there are real problems here and not just a personality conflict. Also, be aware you may not like him, simply because he reminds you of someone you really don't like – that is termed, transference.

Stay calm and carry on

It is essential that you keep an open mind. It might even help to spend more time with your employee - try collaborating on a difficult task, or trying to solve some nagging department problem. I believe that, your perspectives can change by the experiences you have with him.

Also, stay cool and don't wear your emotions on your sleeve. Remain fair, calm, and composed. If you're having trouble with this, talk to another manager who is familiar with the employee's work and see if your impressions match the other manager's.

Finally, check your bias. Think about why you are reacting the way you are and if you have an attitude and perspective based only on liking or disliking someone. This factor can be a major source of dissatisfaction and stress.

When I think back on some of the biggest employee conflicts I had, they were generally with those individuals who challenged me and took me out of a self-imposed comfort zone. Fresh thinking and innovation are often byproducts of some relationship tension, conflict, and agitation.

"Managers Need Employee Ideas and Feedback"

Dear Dave,

The idea of having employees provide ideas and feedback is a great one, but it is laughable, because my company says they want it, but then never use it. Even worse, I have heard one manager tell one of my coworkers, "You just do your job and I'll do all of the thinking." Why would managers say one thing and do another? I have some very

good ideas that could be used, but I am afraid to discuss them.

K

Dear K,

I hear you loud and clear. I think this is a gross violation that happens all too often in organizations. I would even say that it would almost be better for management to say nothing at all about getting ideas and feedback versus 'pulling the rug out' from under well-intentioned workers who want to help.

I once went to my boss with a good idea to help the efficiency of a customer product return process being used and he said, "We kinda like the way things are done." It's funny how some things can never be forgotten.

One recent study surveyed approximately 500 senior executives and managers and a similar number of non-management employees and found that there is a large disconnect between how managers and their workers feel about the communication process.

To recap results, 78% of managers said they demonstrate openness and appreciation for the ideas and opinions of their workers; but just 43% of employees felt this to be true. When asked if they helped guide employees who make mistakes in order to transform failures into learning opportunities, 80% of managers said yes; less than half (47%) of the workers agreed.

You could summarize all this by concluding that, most leaders feel they excel at the behaviors that lead to higher levels of innovation. But, employees don't see their leaders the way leaders see themselves. From the employee viewpoint, leaders struggle to inspire curiosity, challenge deeper perspectives, and create the freedom to innovate.

How to Tap Employee Ideas

Motivation - If you want to get ideas from employees, they need to understand the strategy and purpose of the company. Understanding brings purpose and commitment.

Great Ideas can Come From Anywhere - Stress that revolutionary ideas can come from anywhere and are not just the domain of men and women in lab coats. Employees must believe that everything can be improved and that they can come forward with improvement ideas.

Get the Facts – First and foremost valid data should support and drive ideas and decision making. Most managers will shoot down suggestions that don't take into account all the variables, which is then a huge turn-off for the contributors.

Ask Questions and Give Feedback - A great place to start is to look at your corporate objectives and pick "wicked and nagging" business problems that are bothering everyone. Collectively ask tough questions about why they are happening. Then use the best ideas and collaboratively figure out the solutions.

Free-flowing Communication - The old suggestion box just doesn't do it anymore and surveys take time. Ideas come from the interplay and free exchange of dialogue amongst employees. Look for and create opportunities for employees to get together and brainstorm.

Open the Door - Keeping an open door builds trust and demonstrates an active interest in what employees have to say. Over time, employees will share their ideas as they appear, knowing that a willing listener is waiting to hear them."

"Hanging On to Good Employees"

Dear Dave,

One of my best employees told me she is leaving to work for another company. I had no clue this was coming. I thought she was happy. How can I hang on to my best employees?

M

Dear M,

Many managers use exit interviews to find out why employees are leaving their jobs. Unfortunately, asking an employee on their last day why they are leaving doesn't provide useful information in time to prevent the departure.

An effective approach that some of my Rochester colleagues recommend is a "stay interview." I call it a "hold on to them interview," because it occurs before there is any hint that an employee is about to say goodbye. A stay interview also helps you understand why employees stay, so that those important factors can be reinforced with others.

Defined, a "stay interview" is a periodic one-on-one discussion between a manager and a highly valued "potential-of-leaving employee" that identifies and then reinforces the factors that may compel an employee to stay. It also identifies and minimizes any changeable factors that might cause them to consider quitting.

The stay interview should not be used to intimidate the employee. It's really a conversation that you're having with your employees about their wellbeing and contentment. But, be aware that these interviews may uncover unpleasant truths, such as bad feelings toward management, or other employees. It is crucial that you separate emotions from the facts.

Benefits of "stay" interviews

A stay interview is principally designed to discover why a current employee continues to work for the company, what motivates and engages them, and why they might want to stay with the organization, rather than searching for, or taking, a new position.

You can also use stay interviews to touch base with high-performing employees long before they might decide to leave your company. The focus and purpose of these interviews is to find out what is most motivating them to stay with you and what attractive factors might potentially entice them to work for someone else.

Stay interviews can and should be conversational, casual, and informal, as long as you feel you're gathering honest opinions that will help you create a more attractive work environment. Some tactics for conducting stay interviews include:

Show concern – Be sincere, engaging, and listen a great deal when conducting the interviews. The truth is, most employees are excited simply by the fact that the organization is concerned about their future and that their manager took the time to talk to them.

Personalization – Many companies use stuffy, structured engagement and motivation surveys that are focused on learning what engages a large number of employees. Try customizing the conversation, so it doesn't seem like a (snore) scripted survey – appeal to the individuals and their wants.

Get specifics – Tactfully encourage employees to identify actions that can improve the employee experience and also actions that can help eliminate any major workplace "pain points." Draw out and carefully listen to potentially telling and usable engagement and retention ideas.

Focus on the positive – Most of the dialogue should be focused on identifying and then reinforcing the positive factors that the employee – hopefully - enjoys about their job. These factors should be discussed and highlighted as the reasons the employee chose to work for the company in the first place.

Try to conduct your stay interviews with employees at least once per year, scheduling them separately from performance reviews, so the goals of each remain distinct. Make the stay interviews welcome opportunities to discuss and share ideas.

"Shared Purpose Drives Collaboration"

Dear Dave,

I have a common management problem. How can I get my employees to collaborate more and work together better, instead of just being independent workers, who seem to do their work in isolation?

T

Dear T,

Management theorists believe that team cohesion results from a deep sense of "we-ness," or the pride and bond developed when belonging to a team as a whole. By becoming enthusiastically involved in the efforts of the team, and by recognizing a sense of shared purpose exists among team members, more collaboration is formed.

I wholeheartedly believe that a sense of shared purpose will create team cohesion. Without a sense of purpose, work is a chore rather than an opportunity for success. Employees will rally and support each other – dare I say, think together – if they believe in their mission and have a collective view of significant things they are trying to accomplish.

The goal is to get a lot of people to want to bring their creativity together and accomplish something more important than they can do on their own. Visionary leaders spend their time capitalizing on the opportunity to build cohesive cultures by inspiring people to gather, support and trust each other, and move forward to tackle wicked problems.

Constructing collaboration

Purpose drives goals and the intent to achieve them. People are also driven by a clear definition of the goals and an overarching, motivating purpose - they need to see how their collaboration would benefit a cause larger than that of any individual or team.

Purpose deals with why the organization exists in the first place and what ultimately matters in its work. Business consultant, Lee Colan states in Inc. magazine, your purpose needs to answer the most fundamental question, "Why do we do what we do?" Then, you must answer the fundamental four questions that every employee asks:

Where are we going? *(Goals)*

What are we doing to get there? *(Plans)*

How can I contribute? *(Roles)*

What's in it for me? *(Rewards)*

Leaders must also provide their people a clear, motivating sense of urgency to a cause - a compelling reason to be a part of what the company is doing and why things should be done carefully, but swiftly. People find all kinds of reasons not to work together when they are unclear about, or indifferent to, causes that matter.

Purpose drives strategy

Almost any manager can tell you the company mission and vision (usually framed nicely on the wall), and a few can tell you their company values. But, I think those are almost worthless in their ability to drive the actions of employees, if managers and staff cannot articulate, reflect on, and live a shared purpose.

Recent research suggests that lack of understanding around purpose can lead to demotivation and emotional detachment, which in turn lead to a disengaged and dissatisfied workforce. Clearly, purpose, values, goals, resources, and strategy must be defined and aligned by leadership to drive performance and employee well-being.

While organizational research identifies the importance of communications and leadership in developing a sense of shared purpose, what emerges – and this is crucial - is that employees believe that their leaders must clearly demonstrate that they, too, live the values and purpose they espouse.

In summary, show your staff that, working with a group of people towards common, understood goals can be an extremely rewarding experience. Sell your staff on the fact that, knowing how to collaborate effectively takes commitment and hard work, but the payoffs are substantial – the results create job security.

"Positive Discussions Create Positive Outcomes"

Dear Dave,

It is that time of year when I hold quarterly reviews with my employees. My fellow managers tend to think that the reviews should be an opportunity to "let people have it," as one manager puts it. I want my employees to learn from the reviews and not have the crap scared out of them. I have good employees, though, they all can improve.

T

Dear T,

First, let me say that, I applaud you for conducting quarterly reviews. I hear so many horror stories from friends, colleagues, and students regarding the fact they receive no reviews at all.

Managers owe it to their employees to honestly, sincerely, and constructively appraise the work of their staff. However, providing harsh criticism only isn't the best route. I believe everyone wants to improve themselves and this requires both positive and realistically-negative feedback on their work.

Research shows

I know that, many managers may think that Dave is way too "soft" when dealing with employees. But, psychologists and management researchers have long-known that positive-focused conversations - ones centered on dreams, ambitions, strengths, and possibilities - generate positive emotions and better attitudes about self-improvement.

In turn, these feelings can motivate any one of us to work harder. I believe people innately want to improve themselves. This means, the more positive and constructive the discussion, the more positive the outcome.

Depending on what motivation research you read, most experts believe that employees are more motivated by personal factors than they are by money. Some theorists believe – as I do – that employees crave mastery of what they do, a sense of purpose in their work, and the notion they are contributing to the productivity of the organization as well as helping others succeed.

I sum up all of the motivation research by stating that, from my experience, employees want to feel good about themselves, their work, their peers, their destiny, and their abilities. Accordingly, our appraisals of their behaviors and performance should measure their standing in these areas – not just how many widgets they produced or sold.

Crucial and positive conversations

Managers must assess the different areas of an employee's job. So, what should be on the inventory of items to measure, assess, and discuss? Some of the areas to assess are: dependability, technical skills, adaptability, people skills, team skills, dedication, creativity, personal development, and organizational skills.

During the review it is important for managers to be specific with comments, so that the employee truly knows their strengths and weaknesses. In addition, every review should be a planning opportunity to set realistic goals for improvement, as well as for having a discussion about how the employee's strengths can be increased and exploited.

Remember, constructive feedback is information-specific, issue-focused, and based on actual observations. Be direct when delivering your message, but be sincere and avoid giving vague and mixed messages. In positive feedback situations, express appreciation. In negative feedback situations, express concern. Finally, give the feedback person-to-person, not through e-mail

A caution: When giving negative feedback - especially when a negative incident happens, that upsets you - you may want to take time to cool off and get your thoughts in order before you give the negative feedback.

In conclusion, be observant and acknowledge real performance. Try to catch and respond to employees doing things well, just as much as you catch and respond to them doing something wrong. And, don't acknowledge how they are performing only once or twice a year – feedback should occur almost daily.

"Urgency Can Motivate Employees"

Dear Dave,

I manage a team of 12 people. My problem is, we seem to delay everything and we never seem to take action on big growth opportunities. However, we are great at having meetings. I blame myself, because I can't seem to get my employees to want to make big things happen beyond everyday work demands. Any advice will help.

A

Dear A,

I love your comment about being great at meetings. I have worked with "meeting experts" who were fabulous business gathering planners, but could delay taking action on anything that hinted at commitment and execution.

What you have going there is a "lack of a sense of urgency" problem. This means that anything and everything can be tabled for light years, because there is no pressure or need to act quickly and decisively. This is a huge problem, especially considering that business thrives on execution, speed, and completion.

Urgency is a friend

Too often people think that their job is to complete only their daily task list. If they do so, they think they have actually accomplished something. Yes, tasks are necessary, but may not constitute effectiveness and achievement. Simply, big opportunities require big moves, fueled by change, and driven by a sense of urgency.

I believe there are two basic motivators: fear and desire. These two motivators are experienced by organizations. However, fear or anxiety often creates panic and self-protection (CYA). The other is driven by big opportunities and can create momentum and buy-in. To exploit opportunities – for revenue enhancement or hitting productivity targets - an organization must be driven by passion and desire.

Accordingly, opportunity-driven urgency can create powerful and sustainable action - it can inspire people to be proactive and think beyond what their jobs require of them. Management must make the opportunity real and clear, and thoroughly communicate a doable plan to rally support.

People must understand the goals and outcomes before they can work toward them.

Too often, initiatives and plans are "shoved down people's throats" and employees don't have a chance to digest, interpret, or get their arms around the initiative. The "why" must clearly be defined. In addition, some overzealous managers think everything is a "red flag" urgent item making employees suffer "priority shock." Priorities must be priorities and employees must understand the order of things and what absolutely must take place when.

What to do?

A sense of urgency demands that a company and its employees examine individual and team tasks and activities to determine what makes sense and what is mindless non-sense. Routines and assumptions must be questioned. You cannot blame people for not getting pumped about doing things that seem to add no value.

Leadership expert, Jon Kotter believes that, a sense of urgency around a big opportunity can create powerful and sustainable action. However, the opportunity must be compelling and it must be described and communicated in ways that people can relate to – it must draw on their feelings, passions, and enthusiasm, not just their intellects.

I advise you to set realistic deadlines, setting a minimum time to work on something. I don't know how we ever got into this "last minute execution" mindset, where people believe they do their best work when pressured at the last minute, but you must persuade your workers that the best work is achieved when they dig in early.

It's amazing what power that can be generated when you get a group of excited employees finding creative ways to use that idea to ignite passion in their colleagues, and make change happen.

"Communication is Vital for Change"

Dear Dave,

Here is another question about managing change. As a manager, my job is to make change happen, plain and simple. However, communication is always a problem and I never seem to connect with the employees who need information most – at least that's what I hear. Any suggestions?

R

Dear R,

I never get tired of receiving questions about change, and especially about communication strategies to make change happen. The fact that you are hearing about communication problems is a bad sign, but it may not be entirely your fault. Communication takes at least two individuals and someone else may not be holding up their end of the deal.

I always say that you cannot over-communicate when you are asking your organization or teams to change. I am reminded of the quotation – forget who said it – "There is no such thing as too much information, just poorly presented information."

Few of us have worked in organizations where employees were completely happy with the communication structures. Just when you think you have good communication practices in hand, something goes wrong and people start complaining. However, the fact is, change thrives on communication, so good systems of communication must be implemented.

Possible solutions

Research shows that, not having effective communication means and methods in place is considered by employees to be the number one problem at their places of work – a close second is inept management, but that is a different topic for another time. The good news is, change management practitioners have provided a vast array of suggestions about how to communicate well during any organizational changes.

At the top of their lists is the recommendation to develop a written change management communication plan to ensure that all of the right information gets to the right people at the right times. Yes, a plan!

This means communication gaps and weaknesses must be discovered and a systemic means of providing instructions, information, and feedback must be created and implemented. Here are some other selected communication practices to get and keep people on board:

Explain the why of the change - Pinpoint what exactly is changing and why. Too many change initiatives are loaded with catchy phrases and are short on the substance of what the phrases mean in the day-to-day functional reality of the organization's people. Communicate the reasons for the changes in such a way that people understand the context, the purpose, the urgency, and the need.

Be strategic, but be realistic - Clearly communicate the vision, the mission, and the objectives of the change management initiative. Help people to understand how these changes will affect them professionally and personally. If this is not done, people will make up their own fictitious stories, which are usually more negative than the truth.

Have and articulate ideal outcomes - Know what results you want, ideally, from both the change initiative and the communication program or tactic. Communicate all that is known about the changes, as quickly as the information is available. People fear what they do not understand – help them understand.

Get people interacting and sharing ideas and perspectives - Hold interactive workshops, seminars, and town hall meetings in which all employees can explore the changes together - getting employees involved is crucial. The more people are involved in the process, the fewer you'll have acting as internal curmudgeons, naysayers, and saboteurs.

Finally, listen and give your people multiple opportunities (a clear pipeline) to share concerns, ask questions, and offer ideas - and make following up with answers and updates a top priority for you. Oh … and open your office door, so employees can see that you are open for business.

"Include Critics in Your Planning"

Dear Dave,

Like many companies, we do a lot of planning. As a manager, I have many ideas I want to be heard in our planning sessions. However, when I or anyone else presents ideas, or asks questions that may go against the ideas of upper management, we are considered to be rebels, or we are not being "team players." It is easier to just say nothing and nod our heads. Please write something for managers, who stifle input and ideas.

D

Dear D,

We need more skeptics in planning, so constructive criticism can be heard. Otherwise, you hear and use only narrow-minded, predetermined ideas that often repeat the mistakes of the past, do not use current knowledge and research, and do not use good dialogue and debate to come up with the best plans.

Many managers hate skeptics, because they can derail the "efficiency" of planning. I say, what good is efficient planning, if it does not fit and solve current realities and nagging, wicked problems? The plan must address problems, challenges, and opportunities – and not be something that nurtures egos and is comfortably convenient.

Getting a plan written expeditiously should not be the intent of planning sessions – planning and plan effectiveness and the ability to provide "whole solutions" should be the mission of a planning team. To do this, a plan must be a summative strategy that is composed of many diverse ideas, perspectives, and – dare I say – controversial questions.

Those "nagging critics," who question a quickly-prepared strategy – a plan based only on efficiency and not effectiveness - may be the best source of innovative thinking and problem-solving involved in the planning session. Smart managers welcome tough questions and oppositional thinking from critics when planning.

Managers, please!

When planning, strongly encourage any doubters to speak up, so that people can see what might be wrong with the potential plan. These questions will trigger thoughtful evaluation and push you to seek more alternatives and make the best choices. Creative, innovative ideas come from the generation of questions that challenge popular thinking.

If skeptics have a voice in the process – and if you listen to their feedback – they are far more likely to help conceive of and support a new strategy, and assist in moving it forward. If no one is speaking up about the potential risks of a new strategy, ask your team members to ask: "What would a skeptic worry about here?"

Managers, who surround themselves with "yes people" get exactly what they want – nothing but agreement and shallow thinking. Actually, they get no thinking at all. The old saying, "If everyone is thinking alike, then no one is really thinking" rings all too true in so many planning sessions. If you want valuable, "crazy" solutions, you need diverse, valuable "crazy ideas."

To be clear, I am not suggesting that you have everyone tear into each other and that you end up with a bunch of people who hate each other. I am suggesting that you create an environment and culture where skepticism, criticism, diverse ideas, and oppositional thinking can develop and flourish. In short, the more ideas you have, the better the alternatives you can consider and the better the choices you will make.

Planning should be a fun, rewarding, interactive, and interesting adventure. Nothing makes the staff of a company more proud than believing and knowing their input and ideas matter, and that they had a hand in the planning process, the plan itself, and in the implementation of a shared, effective plan product.

"Accepting Constructive Criticism"

Dear Dave,

As a long-time manager, I believe in providing constructive appraisals of my employees at least twice a year. Unfortunately, at many of these reviews, my employees become quite defensive about what I think are beneficial, constructive suggestions I make regarding their improvement. Often, this defensiveness derails the review. Any suggestions?

M

Dear M,

First, let me say that, if a manager is really doing their job, the performance review should not be a shock to the employee. The employee should know where they stand and how they are doing – good or bad - by almost daily feedback given by the manager.

I do think it is human nature for individuals to coil up in a defensive mode if they feel they are being "attacked" – even in a performance review. It makes me think that maybe it is not always the message, but how the message is communicated.

Accordingly, I believe the problem lies more with the methods we traditionally use to provide feedback, rather than with some shortcoming of the individual responsible for orchestrating the performance conversation.

I'm not blaming you for your employees' defensive nature; I am just stating that there are ways to deliver even bad news about performance in a way that doesn't make the employee resent what you are saying.

Defensiveness 101

As a manager, it is tough to give negative feedback to your people. Their defensiveness can be disturbing, causing you to side-step your intended message. Defensiveness breaks down communication and, often, the performance appraisal interaction ceases.

It is not uncommon for employees to become self-protective and start to rationalize and make excuses for their lack of performance. Ego and self-esteem come into play making employees focus on all the good things they have accomplished, while avoiding discussing their performance weaknesses.

I think employees come into performance reviews with a defensive mindset already working away in their mind. Many times, they are waiting for the old "compliment sandwich," where they know their boss will start out with a compliment, then lower the boom on them, then end with some insincere compliment. Managers, who employ the sandwich technique mean well, but it just doesn't work.

Breaking down defensiveness

To break down barriers, managers should master the art of assertive language, which is based on the premise that you can emphasize what you need to say and still be respectful. In short, don't be wishy-washy - say what you mean, respectfully, but directly.

Managers should also use positive language, and focus on ways to solve problems. Put the focus on the desired performance, rather than pounding on the current negative performance. And never, ever attack personalities; just focus on behaviors and the impact of the behaviors in the performance of the work.

Also, get employees involved early in the process. Initiate a dialogue with the employee that allows him or her to think of their own ways to improve their performance. Allowing the employee to assess her own performance, can greatly decrease the defensive behavior.

Finally, know your mental state going into the performance discussion. You must be calm, rational, and unemotional for the performance discussion to be productive. If you are extremely upset or angry, your attitude will be disrespectful and is likely not to produce the results you want from the appraisal.

Remember, in your role as a leader, employee evaluations are mandatory and can be quite useful Employees need and deserve to know how they are doing. Your goal then is to have the employee hear your constructive message and act positively on it.

"New Managers Must Avoid Mistakes"

Dear Dave,

I am a new manager and I certainly want to do well. I have had some good and some very poor bosses and I think I know what good management is. Do you have any advice for me, such as what to do and not to do?

M

Dear M,

Being promoted to a manager's position does not automatically come with an owner's manual. What should be a natural and human-centered organizational role, management has become – or has been made to become – all too complex by thousands of "experts" (not yours truly, of course).

Most certainly, management is about being a trusted and respected leader, who is there to guide and develop the individuals and teams to their highest potential. It's about establishing positive relationships with those who work for you and thinking and working together to set and achieve tough goals.

You will notice that I bounce back and forth about naming your role as either a manager or a leader. I believe managers must be leaders and I also believe leaders should learn and know how to manage. That is a discussion for another column.

Leaders make their employees want to contribute and pitch in. Leadership is about inspiring staff to prevail, despite the adversity they are facing. Driving employees like rented mules will never get you anywhere. At the end of the day, work is a people business and people have wants, needs, and emotions.

This is crucial: Make sure to ask your staff what they think and always gain their input and observations. Talk to them. Ask them questions. Be sincere and interested in their well-being. Remember, their ideas can be a valuable asset. Here is some more advice for how to best lead your employees.

Good practices

Want to be there. Show your staff that you are excited to be at work, and hopefully they, too, will feel the same way. I think nothing is more discouraging to employees than seeing their peers and managers act like they hate every minute of the work day.

Set goals and priorities together, and gain input on how to complete projects. I believe large pieces of work should be broken down into manageable chunks of work. Doing so allows employees the opportunity to see large goals and projects as an incremental system of doable tasks and not as overwhelming work monsters. Oh … then praise and recognize outstanding work.

Demonstrate trust. It may be hard to do at times, but have trust in all of your staff. Think the best until proven otherwise; trust given is trust returned. And if there is a misunderstanding, take enough time to talk to them directly, instead of addressing any issue by word-of-mouth, or by e-mail.

Don't be a "my way or the highway" type of tyrant. In truth, you don't know everything, so don't act like you do. How else is your staff going to come up with new ideas, learn, and improve if you're busy making sure only your opinion and ideas are the right ones?

Be in the moment and open up your office door. How is anything going to get done with a boss who hides in his or her office all day? Network constantly, establish connections with those around, you and build relationships. This will help set an example for your staff to do the same with their coworkers.

And, do not micro-manage. Your employees do not like smothering and control, and therefore won't take kindly to being told, "Do this…" and "Do that…" while you hover over them like an autocratic drone. Delegate the work and empower people to carry out their assigned tasks.

"Telecommuters Need Motivation, Too"

Dear Dave,

I manage 18 people and I am satisfied with their performance levels. My problem is, my organization wants me to have more of my employees work from home. I am not in favor of this, but it is not my call. How can I be sure that those working from home stay connected and motivated, as well as perform?

T

Dear T,

Most experts agree that it's harder to manage a teleworker than someone sitting in the same office. A big question to answer before letting employees work from home is can you handle it? Can you let go?

World-wide telecommuting has become more common. Management researchers have identified several benefits to working remotely: Mainly, it boosts employee performance and satisfaction and reduces turnover and office costs.

According to a survey done by the Computing Technology Industry Association, 67 percent of survey respondents said their organization has experienced greater worker productivity as a result of allowing employees to telecommute, either full- or part-time. The main reason for the increase in worker output: less commute time.

Tele-Issues

The authors of, "*How to Manage Virtual Teams*," writes that, team member may not naturally know how to interact effectively across space and time. They need strong team skills such as setting goals, sharing responsibility for getting things done, and providing mutual support. And they need smart leadership to make sure they can leverage those skills in a virtual working environment.

Problems can also include: difficulties in communicating and understanding one another; failure to develop processes such as setting clear goals and standards; inability to collaborate in a way that takes advantage of different perspectives, knowledge, and expertise; a lack of full engagement and commitment by all team members to deliver their best work.

Here are some other issues you should consider:

1. 'Cabin Fever" – telecommuters can experience isolation when working from remote sites, removed from interactions. Some companies insist on part-time telecommuting schedules, where workers have set days in the office for meetings or other team events.

2. Tensions can arise when employees don't see one another or understand their colleagues' workloads, and some who must work in the office will feel resentment toward those who can work from home.

3. Telecommuting takes a lot of self-discipline, so somebody has to want to do it and has the ability to work

independently without requiring a lot of face-to-face interaction with managers and coworkers.

4. When employees have limited face-to-face contact, they are less likely to help their co-workers, especially in last-minute or emergency situations.

Tele-Managing

While you don't necessarily need to watch an employee's every mouse click, it's a good idea to set ground rules and make sure that staffers aren't watching "The View" or heading out to go fishing during work hours.

Learn management by objective, or task (results), not by time in seats. Also, keep all team members in close communication and create a collaborative mindset. Creating a sense of team is critical for virtual workers, so they can stay in touch, participate, share ideas, and get to know each other.

Also, clarify the team's purpose, goals, and performance standards. You should also plan regular feedback for the team in a group environment such as a web meeting or conference call, as well as for individuals via phone calls, and e-mails. When possible, occasional face-to-face meetings should be arranged to allow for more personal connections.

Finally, celebrate milestones and successes. Feeling like a team means not just working together but being recognized for team members' sacrifices and accomplishments.

"Bonds Are Needed To Keep Employees"

Dear Dave,

I am a fairly new manager. Our competition is always trying to lure away our best employees. How can we retain our most productive employees? How can we build stronger emotional bonds with them?

T

Dear T,

Simple answer: Treat them right and don't micro-manage the pejeepers out of them. Also, help them grow, achieve, master their craft, and groom them for advancement – if they want it.

A major problem for employers today is attracting the best talent, and then retaining key employees. Research shows that the key ingredient for retention lies within the manager's ability to understand what employees really want.

Talent management and retention is mandatory for your organizations' health. If you are losing critical staff members, you can safely bet that other people in other departments in your company are looking as well.

Realize that the quality of the management an employee receives is critical to employee retention. People leave managers more often than they leave companies or jobs. It is not enough that the manager is well-liked or a nice person. Starting with clear expectations of the employee, the manager has a critical role to play in retention.

What Employees Crave

One recent survey shows some interesting results regarding what managers think employees crave and what employees really want.

What managers think employees want, starting with the most important:

- o Good wages
- o Job Security
- o Promotion and growth opportunities
- o Good working conditions
- o Interesting work
- o Personal loyalty to workers
- o Tactful discipline
- o Full appreciation for work done
- o Sympathetic understanding of personal problems
- o Feeling "in" on things

What employees say they want, starting with the most important:

- o Full appreciation for work done
- o Feeling "in" on things
- o Sympathetic understanding of personal problems
- o Job security
- o Good wages
- o Interesting work
- o Promotion and growth opportunities
- o Personal loyalty to workers
- o Good working conditions
- o Tactful discipline

You can see there is quite a discrepancy. This indicates the value of the "intangible rewards" of appreciation, involvement, and understanding. An important benefit is that the top 3 things employees want are all influenced by the relationship with their direct manager.

Maintaining a positive culture is key in retaining your best employees. Follow these five tips to keep the best workers on staff!

Your Employees Should Feel They are Recognized and Appreciated — Make the effort to praise your employees on a regular basis.

Understand Your Employees' Potential — It's your responsibility to identify the unique talents of your employees and make sure that their assigned duties match their skills.

Offer Awards and Incentives — Spotlight your best employees and offer incentives to keep them engaged and happy.

Keep Employees Challenged — Employees are motivated when they feel challenged in their position. When they are not challenged, they can quickly get bored and are more likely to leave.

Treat Employees with Respect — Morale is affected negatively when you do not show employees the proper respect. Also be sure to thank employees for going the extra mile or acknowledge when you have made a mistake.

Conclusion: Firms that neglect their best workers and hold on to old practices without considering today's changing business climate, risk losing their most important assets.

Companies that pay attention to employee needs and wants - by engaging their employees, cultivating a positive work environment and encouraging a culture of appreciation and recognition - will attract and retain the best employees.

"Recognize Opportunities for Recognition"

Dear Dave,

As a past manager, I think employee recognition is important. What are your beliefs about employee recognition? What are the most creative recognition ideas that you have heard about?

B

Dear B,

My belief is that everyone who does work well should be recognized for it – publicly or privately. Also, there should be consequences for poor performance, but that is another issue outside the realm of your questions.

Let me first say that some people are private and tend to shy away from public displays of recognition. So, be careful, do not march someone in front of their peers and heave a reward on them until you know for sure that doing so would not embarrass them.

As I mention in my book, "Ask Dave" (hint hint), people do want to be appreciated when they work hard on projects and tasks, and it is crucial that managers stay alert for occasions when their employees should be congratulated. I always say, what gets rewarded gets repeated.

Common Recognition

I believe that, most "good companies" will create and support effective recognition programs for both individuals and teams. These companies realize that it is important to show appreciation for their most valuable resource – people. Not rocket surgery, right?

Motivating and recognizing employees is vital to the development of an effective and positive work environment, and it is common for companies to use traditional forms of recognition to show their appreciation for work well done such as bonuses, plaques, and prizes.

In many organizations recognition and financial reward are linked. An employee does something above and beyond "normal job expectations" and receives a gift card or a lunch with the boss (some may not consider lunch with the boss a reward), or a team achieves a goal and is rewarded with a party.

Often, company recognition programs have a name, a theme, and a plan of expectations, milestones, and rewards. Employees get pumped up, managers are given goals, and everyone is off to the races. Seriously, these programs are important – I don't mean to belittle them – I just think that all too often, "cookie cutter" programs are more sizzle than steak and the point and impact of the recognition itself gets lost in the regimented format of the program.

Recognition 2.0

As much as I think it is important to give people things for good work, I think it is more effective and more appreciated by the employees if managers would spend more time just thanking people for small and large achievements each and every day. I don't see why management has to wait until the calendar says it is time to show someone appreciation.

Smart management wanders about and catches people doing good things, then appreciates them in some way for that work. I remember a boss of mine writing a thank you on a sticky note and tacking it on my computer screen when I was away. When I saw it, I was elated.

However, there are those companies that believe all of this recognition stuff is nonsense and people will thrive only on their paychecks. Further, the management of these companies will not even come up to one of their employees to say something like, "Hey, Fred, good job!" Even dogs get bones. OK, I feel better having said this.

Any manager can make a positive difference in their workplace culture by noticing and appreciating the efforts of the people they manage. I truly believe that employees care more for and remember most those small, sincere, and personal expressions of gratitude made by their manager to them.

"Maintaining Motivation in Troubling Times"

Dear Dave,

I am a manager for a company in Rochester that appears to be losing interest in sustaining a presence and workforce here. Needless to say, my employees are quite nervous about the uncertainty this is causing. I want my employees to remain committed and be enthused about their work, but this is becoming increasingly difficult. Any advice?

R

Dear R,

First, let me say that no company's future is completely secure and every employee wonders what news or actions are coming down the pike. However, even if it appears that your organization is moving or downsizing, you can still help your team members stay focused, positive, and deliver results.

Working under fear of the future and wondering about the stability of a company is demotivating. It's no wonder those who are fearful of losing their jobs, or overwhelmed with the prospect of taking on more responsibilities, can quickly become demoralized, stifling productivity and well-being.

It's difficult for a leader to stay positive and strong when dealing with uncertainty and the possibility a company may say adios to the staff. However, your employees are watching your lead, so make sure you appear to be determined, focused, strategic, and communicative no matter what is going on.

Please also keep in mind that you can see challenging times as an opportunity or as a threat. If you see it as an opportunity, this will impact how you respond and your actual results. It is crucial that you and your team focus time and energy on delivering results to your usual high standards, rather than getting caught up on negativity and complacency.

Some morale-building tactics

I think creating and effectively communicating a compelling vision is a vital leadership role.

This is why successful leaders also reinforce values in their communications. Shared values provide direction during times of uncertainty, comfort during periods of difficult change, and inspiration in the face of adversity.

The importance of communicating - and listening more - during difficult times is extremely crucial. Even though communicating through technology is increasingly common, it never replaces face-to-face communication. Work on making an effort to connect personally with your employees, particularly when you sense times are most difficult. This not only reduces misunderstandings, but it builds trust. In short, don't hide; your staff wants lots of dialogue, honesty, and as much information as possible.

Showing respect is critical. I think you should ask for input and respect the opinions you receive, while acknowledging results and expressing gratitude - leaders must recognize the impact of their tough decisions and show appreciation to people for their efforts and sacrifices.

Good leaders also steer attention away from fear and uncertainty and toward a renewed purpose by describing clear, achievable, short-term goals (where the organization is going and steps to get there). Celebrating even small victories are particularly important in difficult times. Also, it's beneficial to emphasize results hoped for this month, rather than next year.

Be as honest as you possibly can. Whatever you know, share it with your employees. Don't try to protect people from the truth, or ignore what's happening. In tough situations, people are on high alert for lies and inauthentic messages.

If cutbacks occur, be visible and be clear about your expectations. I believe you should inform all remaining employees about the situation as quickly as possible and, preferably, in person. Carefully explain why such a difficult decision was required and acknowledge the impact on staff. Then, provide an opportunity for employees to express their feelings and their concerns.

Finally, I think people want to believe their work matters in any situation. Give your team a larger purpose. To keep people focused, give them something to work toward. Identify a profound collective purpose and communicate it often.

"Things that Actually Motivate Employees"

Dear Dave,

I am in a management role and our organization has become an increasingly stressful place to work. I have good employees and I want them to be motivated and happy. Please suggest some ways I can motivate them. I don't have a budget for cash rewards, so I hope there are other ways.

B

Dear B,

I feel your pain. And I am one of those people who believes money is not much of a sustainable motivator –

though people do need money. I just believe there are better ways to inspire and engage your employees.

We do know – and especially in this trying economy - there are no promises that anyone's job will last forever. This adds to workplace stress. To alleviate stress and become more motivated, employees must possess a love of their work, a sense of community nurturing their individuality, and frequent messages from leaders that tell employees what they do matters to so many others.

Accordingly – and as I have written in the past – the people that are most happy in their work are often found in mission-driven organizations led by leaders that make employees feel like they have positive impact on social needs and the greater good. In short, when people contribute and believe they are making positive differences, they are happiest.

My belief is that well-intentioned managers tend to make too big a chore out of employee motivation. I think you can boil down employee motivation to one basic strategy: finding out what your employees want and finding a way to give it to them, or to enable them to earn it.

Motivation methods

Harvard professor, Rosabeth Moss Kanter summarizes the keys to strong work motivation in three Ms - mastery, membership, and meaning. Money is a distant fourth. Kanter also believes money must be adequate or fair, but compensation runs out of steam quickly as a source of sustained performance. Kanter says leaders at all levels can focus on the following:

Mastery: Help people develop skills and get better and better at what they do. People innately want to get better at what they do and being challenged by difficult goals helps to develop their talents. Even in the most seemingly routine areas, when people are given difficult problems to tackle - with appropriate and tools and support - they desire to do things faster, smarter, and better.

Membership: Align individuality with community. Community solidarity and bonding comes from employees using their individual talents in concert with those of others in challenging team assignments. Leaders can give employees frequent opportunities to meet people across the organization to help them get to know one another more deeply and work on some nagging problems, or opportunities for progress.

Meaning: Articulate and reinforce a larger purpose. Purpose is the "why" the company is doing what it is doing. Leaders can emphasize the positive impact of the work employees do in supporting the mission of the company. I believe people want and need to see how their work has impact on the company's final products and services, and its customers.

Management writer, Daniel Pink echoes Kanter's beliefs with a similar set of motivators: autonomy, mastery, and purpose. He describes autonomy as a desire to be effective and to be left alone (empowered) to get the work done. Pink argues against old models of motivation driven by rewards and fear of punishment – carrot or stick.

At the end of the day, highly-engaged people who contribute more of themselves can produce astounding things that win customers, build community, or build innovations that change the world. Leaders have tough jobs, but they need to get employee motivation right.

"Managers Can Be Abusive and Abused"

Dear Dave,

You respond to a lot of questions about abusive managers, but how about when managers are abused by their workers? Where I work, our manager is constantly being abused and undermined by a few employees and human resources will do nothing about it, or even back up our manager. I feel bad for him and it seems like there is nothing he can do.

M

Dear M,

If I was your manager, the first thing I would do is write up the employees for insubordination and hunt around your place of work looking for some reasonable upper manager to hear my case. I am not sure why this is allowed to happen, but it must be put to a stop, right away.

If an employee abuses a manager and refuses to carry out directives, typical recourses available to the abused manager include talking to the employee to resolve the abuse, disciplinary action, terminating the employee, or transferring the employee.

Typically, in a situation such as yours, the manager often terminates the employee. Exceptions include settings such as government and some educational areas where terminating an employee is difficult. Most companies have a termination process, such as 3 strikes and you are history.

According to one of my MBA management professors, employees are required to obey company directives issued by their supervisor or manager. A refusal to obey a supervisor's order or a lack of respect directed toward that supervisor will subject that employee to the company's progressive step discipline program.

Act Decisively

I know it's tough to confront bad behavior, but if a manager doesn't it'll erode the credibility and the respect of his or her other employees. Failure to confront abusive employees emboldens bad behavior by others. It tells them that the manager is weak, afraid, and incompetent.

Trust me, anyone behaving badly at work has successfully behaved badly elsewhere. That mean's they've had plenty of practice, know how and when to act out, and look forward to the rewards that go with it. They are experts at causing trouble.

Abusive employees are twisted thinkers and – as I wholeheartedly believe – suffer from lousy self-esteem. They get great satisfaction in just watching your manager squirm by undermining him with other employees. This is bullying - it must be kyboshed!

As I mentioned, all too quickly, insubordinate behavior by one employee can cause a drop in departmental morale and it can give the impression that the manager is losing control of employees.

Necessary Steps

There are steps that a manager should follow before confronting employee insubordination. Losing control by reacting emotionally is the wrong response and that can cause one to make the wrong decision. Also, the abusive employees crave the fact that they made the manager lose control.

There are times when this situation can be "nipped in the bud" with a brief word or corrective discussion. But, when faced with repeated instances of inappropriate behavior, managers must enforce formal discipline programs.

My advice to managers is that termination may, in fact, be the appropriate response to an insubordinate employee, but don't fire the employee on the spot. If termination is appropriate, it will still be clearly appropriate after you've cooled off. Being abusive in return is never appropriate.

So, what needs to be clearly communicated throughout the organization is the simple fact that the refusal to perform to 'reasonable' orders is cause for termination. Incorporating this practice into the daily routine requires discipline and consistency on behalf of the manager.

"Employee Reviews Are Crucial"

Dear Dave,

Where I work, managers are' forced' to give employee performance reviews. My manager came right out and said, she didn't like doing them and thought they were a waste of time. I think it is only right that we receive reviews to let us know how we are doing. What are your thoughts?

M

Dear M,

I fully agree with you. I think employees deserve to receive reviews and most – like you – want to know how they are performing – especially when they know they are doing a great job.

I am not sure what happened, but performance reviews have become, or have always been, some arduous chore for many managers. Granted, they take time, consideration, and planning, but, hey, that's their job, man!

The employee performance review is, theoretically, designed to be a conversation of sorts, where the manager has the opportunity to present what they see and the employee gets the chance to discuss and think about how they are performing. That's the theory any way.

Goals of Employee Performance Evaluation

Managers tell me it is crucial that the employee and the supervisor are both clear about the employee's goals, required outcomes or outputs, and how the success of the contributions will be assessed. Simply, what should the employee be doing and how will their work get measured?

I believe the goals of the best employee performance evaluations are also employee development and organizational improvement goals. The employee performance evaluation helps employees accomplish both personal development needs and has an opportunity to see how they fit into the larger organizational goals.

It is interesting that the very act of writing down the goals takes the employee one step closer to accomplishing them, because they feel like they 'own the goals'. Also, it is only right that employees have their goals documented and available for reference.

Further, if goals, deliverables, and measurements are negotiated – yes, I said negotiated - in an effective employee performance evaluation, the employee and the supervisor are more committed to achieving them. The written personal development goals should also become a commitment from the organization to assist the employee to grow in his or her career.

Some may argue with me, but I believe *everyone* wants to develop and grow at work. I find it hard to believe that personal growth opportunities will not motivate people. Accordingly, managers must capitalize on this basic need and do everything they can to nurture the development of employee skills and abilities.

From a Legal Standpoint

One lawyer I know tells me that, employee performance evaluation provides legal, ethical, and visible evidence that employees were actively involved in understanding the requirements of their jobs and their performance. The accompanying goal setting, performance feedback, and documentation ensure that employees understand their required outputs.

Also, from a legal standpoint, the employee performance evaluation provides evidence of non-discriminatory **promotion**, pay, and recognition processes. This is an important consideration in training managers to perform consistent, regular, non-discriminatory employee performance evaluations. The documentation of success and failure to achieve goals is a critical component of the employee performance evaluation process.

In conclusion: Employees want to know how they are doing and what they should be doing; managers need to get things done; and the company will survive only if goals are fulfilled.

"The Best Managers Develop Their Employees"

Dear Dave,

As a manager, I am concerned about developing my employees. I have some talented people who could use additional training and skill development, but, I hate to say that my company is not generous with the time or money needed to help develop and grow our staff. Please write something about the value of investing in the growth of the employees.

R

Dear R,

Simply, companies need responsive, innovative thinkers and problem-solvers and this is not possible without the building block of learning and development in the firm.

Unfortunately, in many organizations, training budgets are dependent on the health of the company. When things are going well, training is given budgetary considerations. But, when times are tough, companies tend to slash training budgets – along with good people.

In any economic environment, the training expense should be determined by your strategy and goals, not just by other budget-related factors. I believe training people will get you more of what you want and cutting dollars in human resource development is quite costly in the long run. In short, you can't achieve desired results if your workers don't have the required know-how.

Why employee growth should be a top concern

There are numerous benefits of investing in employee training and development, including increased job satisfaction, motivation, and morale among employees. In addition, more motivated workers increase productivity for increased earnings. Also, motivated staff means lower overall turnover and absenteeism.

I can hardly think of anything more important than planning the development of your staff. Yet, all too commonly, training is ignored, or given low priority status, because it is hard to pin a dollar value on the results of training. However, companies that do not train aggressively will see the inevitable costs - the loss of talented workers.

Learning is crucial for sustained growth and stability. Employees are the ones that produce, innovate, deal with customers, and deliver and manage your products or services every day. With the changes and challenges present in the modern marketplace, continual learning is critical to your business's continued success and for the development of future leaders.

As a downside, training does take time. Employees miss out on work time while attending training sessions, which may create some temporary productivity gaps and delay the completion of projects. Despite these drawbacks, training and development provides both the company as a whole and the individual employees with benefits that make the cost and time far exceed the investment.

It is the manager's job

The best managers try to capitalize on employee strengths, interests, growth aspirations, and passions to create greater value for the firm. There is an obvious link between organizational performance and the fulfillment of individual development goals. Savvy managers look for developmental opportunities and they regularly discuss skill development needs with their team members.

Accordingly, employees' direct (mostly mid-level) managers are often the most important talent developers. These managers are closest to the actual work the employees are doing and can easily spot skill gaps and training needs. However, there must be a commitment by management to constantly be on the prowl for training opportunities.

Staff development doesn't have to be complicated, elaborate, or costly. Basically, it's mostly a matter of good managers taking the time to recognize and understand their employee' skills needs and then devising a plan to get staff up to speed on how to best do their job.

In conclusion, your employees are your principle business asset. Good talented people naturally want to advance, and appreciate meaningful support in the process. Grow your employees, thoughtfully and strategically, and you'll reap rewards that pay off now and for years to come.

"Reward the Right Team Behaviors"

Dear Dave,

How can I best recognize and reward my teams? I know that individual employees believe they are incentivized well at our company, but I need the teams to collaborate more, hit team targets, and feel like they are rewarded as a group. Ideas?

M

Dear M,

It appears you are rewarding individual performance well, but, yes, it's critical to reward and recognize your team collectively.

Studies have found that the principal motivator for employee performance is recognition of a job well done and people would much rather work for an employer that recognizes their efforts, rather than only giving feedback when they have done something wrong! That seems obvious, eh?

Although the idea of rewarding workers beyond their pay and benefits package seems necessary, some leaders avoid the practice, because: they may not know how to reward teams versus just individuals; they don't have the time to do it; or, perhaps, because they feel uncomfortable praising people openly.

This is unfortunate, because these problems reduce team performance, and all of these problems can be solved, or should be avoided. Simply, the most successful leaders are those who recognize and reward their team's efforts – often and sincerely. This not only builds trust, but it strengthens team bonds – and turnover is often much lower in teams that have a strong bond with their leader.

Meaningful team rewards are crucial, because it's becoming harder for organizations to find the people they need - finding and keeping talented people requires rewards that motivate and express sincere gratitude for performance. Even the most self-directed and self-motivated employees and teams need praise, recognition, and a "pat on the back."

Rewarding teams

Appropriately rewarding team members for something they've done well takes some investigation and effort on your part. If you don't put much thought into what you're doing, then you may just upset the people you're trying to thank. This is why you should sit down with your team, discuss incentives, and find out how they'd really like to be rewarded.

I believe managers do not need to make the team reward process too complicated, and one of the best ways to make a group of people feel recognized and appreciated is a simple, but genuine, "Thank you." Timing is everything, so catch your teams doing things right and tell them thanks right away.

Something else that most people appreciate is more time off – giving staff a day off for big project successes, or allowing them to leave work an hour early on a Friday afternoon if they finish their work before the set deadline are great rewards and motivators. Some managers will think this is impossible to do, but I think it is far cheaper and more practical than letting your best people say, "Adios."

Some managers use formal systems of recognition and reward linked to salaries, bonuses, and promotions, but, obviously, this requires much more management and monitoring to be effective, and also costs more money. In order for such a system to be effective, it needs to be transparent, desired, and fair to the employees.

Please make sure that, every time you praise people on your team, be specific about what they did to deserve the recognition. Being specific not only tells the team exactly what they did, it also lets the whole team know that you're paying attention and care. So, specify why the work made a positive difference and contribution.

Finally, think about using tasteful, meaningful, and well-timed thank you notes (thank you, Jimmy Fallon). Don't over-do them and water down their impact. These small gestures of recognition are powerful and their payoffs are enormous.

"Build Networks for Change"

Dear Dave,

At my company, we are involved in many change efforts. My fellow managers seem to want to force change upon their employees, but I think there must be better ways to implement changes. Any ideas?

T

Dear T,

Yes, and the first idea I have is to create sound change communities, instead of adversaries, which is often caused by forcing people to accept change strategies without first selling the value of the change strategies. Simply, alliances work better than shoving orders down people's throats.

The Influence Test

I believe the difference between a leader who can successfully manage and implement change and one who can't is often the effectiveness of their sphere of influence and relationships, and knowing who the core influencers are. To assess your potential for influencing change, ask yourself these questions:

> **Approachability** - Do people come to me for work-related advice and assistance? When employees approach you and rely on you, it signals that they trust you and respect your competence, wisdom, and leadership. The more they turn to you, the more influence you have for change to occur.
> **Linkage** - Are my employees well-connected to one another? This is advantageous, because it leads to a cohesive network with high levels of trust and support. Information and ideas are spread and validated through multiple channels, so it's easier to coordinate the group.
> **Resistance** - Who within my sphere of influence is doubtful, resistant, or strongly opposed to a proposed

change? Do some inquiry and ask questions - both direct and indirect - to gauge change acceptance. Then, analyze and act on your observations.

Persuasion - What is the context (conditions and background) for change? Is there a way to tell a simple and compelling story to everyone – especially the most well-connected employees - about why change management is essential and not a mindless change strategy du jour?

To communicate change, you must speak the language of your employees. You can build credibility by telling a compelling story of change management in a new way that makes sense. Bear in mind, it is human nature for us to resist change when it is thrust upon us, even if that change is in our best interest. We do not like actions that are done **to** us.

A Network of Change Champions

Effective change management must be systemic. This requires leaders, who are skilled in driving and selling change, as well as building organizational capability to manage and sustain the implementation and momentum of change.

Gaining employee buy-in and support for a change initiative is best achieved by staff engagement. By "engagement" I mean not only communications, but active participation by the people who have a vested interest in the outcome of the change initiative.

Leaders will also gain momentum and positive support for change by building an internal network of "change champions." A change champion network is a group of respected key individuals, well positioned across the organization, who will speak well of the change and provide positive word-of-mouth to doubtful or resistant people.

Change champions help reduce the inevitable ambiguity and uncertainty associated with implementing change. Additionally, these change champions can serve as role models executing key change tasks. Change champions are skilled at initiating, selling, facilitating, and implementing change.

Finally, it is crucial that leaders select and train the right people to act as change champions. Leaders must make sure they are clear about what they are expecting from the change champions, what change results are needed, and how they will be rewarded.

"Management Styles Are Developed"

Dear Dave,

I had a job interview recently and one of the questions was, "How would you describe your management style?" I have managed employees for a long time, but I guess I really never considered whether or not I had a style; I just did what I thought was right and what good managers do. Please write something about management styles.

R

Dear R,

I like your style – you wrote to me. Managers have to perform many roles in an organization and how they handle various situations and people will depend on their style of management. A management style is considered an overall and consistent method and system of leadership used by a manager.

Management styles are also characteristic ways of making decisions and relating to employees. I could write volumes about the importance of effective management styles and the many styles managers may develop, but I will try to cut to the chase.

The basics

Let me first say that, the best managers earn respect by giving respect to their employees. This shows they value their employees as individuals and performers – a feeling that in all likelihood will be mutual. This style never gets stale.

Also, good managers build an environment of trust. Trust exists when an employee can say they know they can make a mistake at work without being criticized or fired – but, they are expected to learn from their mistakes.

Good managers are good leaders

Managers must be involved, engaged, and analytical leaders. Good leaders can read and adapt to the unique demands of the situation, the needs of the people involved, and the particular challenges facing the organization.

Emotional Intelligence guru, Daniel Goleman, describes six different styles of leadership. The most effective leaders can move among these styles, adopting the one that meets the needs of the moment. These styles can all become part of the leader's arsenal of performance.

The **Visionary** style is most appropriate when an organization needs a new direction- the goal is to move people towards a new set of shared aspirations and dreams. This leader believes that, explaining the "why" will produce the "how."

The **Coaching** style is a one-on-one highly-participatory style and focuses on developing individuals, showing them how to improve their performance, and helping to connect their goals to the goals of the organization - without micromanaging them.

An **Affiliating style** emphasizes the importance of team work, and creates harmony in a group by connecting people to each other, heightening team cohesion and increasing morale. Managers who embrace this style are concerned with employees' feelings, thoughts, and wellbeing.

A **Democratic** style draws on people's knowledge and skills, and creates group commitment to the company mission. This style gathers and appreciates diverse opinions and ideas, and achieves consensus before reaching a final decision.

With a **Pacesetting** style, the leader is task-oriented and sets high standards for performance. This style is obsessive about doing things better and faster, and asks the same of everyone. These leaders are highly involved in the day-to-day work and are fully aware of operations and procedures.

Finally, the **Commanding** style is an autocratic one and a classic model of "military" style leadership – probably the most often used, but the least often effective. However, some employees do deserve this leadership style. But, because it rarely involves praise and frequently employs criticism, it can hurt the morale and job satisfaction of the best employees.

In conclusion, while elements of personal style may vary, and no matter what you decide about your own style, you should give it some careful thought, because it is always better to manage with sensitivity, authenticity, and sincerity.

Chapter 3 –
Managers/Bosses from Hell

Do you have a bad boss? I know I had several. Almost everyone does have a bad boss at one time or another. In fact, never encountering a bad boss during your whole career progression would be quite lucky. They are everywhere!

A bad boss is a significant factor and a very important force in most people's lives. We know, though, that not every bad boss screams at and threatens employees – some are that notorious and spiteful passive-aggressive type. And, I hate to say this, odds are that if you have a bad boss, you may accidently start picking up of his or her traits and behaviors. The old adage is, "You tend to manage the way you were managed." This means that, if you have a bad boss, run, hide, stay away from him or her.

Now, get this: According to the Workplace Bullying and Trauma Institute, an abusive boss is more likely to be a woman than a man. That's right -- forget that motherly, nurturing image. Woman to woman bullying represents 50 percent of all workplace bullying; man to woman is 30 percent, man to man 12 percent and woman to man bullying is extremely rare -- only 8 percent.

Hopefully, most of your bosses are competent, kind, and even, worthy of your trust and respect. Unfortunately, too often, employees have difficult bosses who impact their desire to engage and contribute at work. It is no surprise that employees who quit their job are most frequently leaving their bosses, not necessarily the company or their job.

Let's take a look at two forms of leadership and see what may result:

Bad Leadership - Workers learn no more than necessary to do their job. It is difficult to recognize natural talent when the job is to follow orders without input. Unique ability is lost to the employee and the company.

Visionary Leadership - Workers have continuous learning opportunity with decision-making responsibility. Employees, with natural talent are quickly recognized and their unique skill is quickly adapted to the organization. As a result - efficiency of the workplace increases.

I think you get the idea about why visionary leadership trumps bad leadership. I would also say there are two kinds of bad bosses: One doesn't know they're bad – they just are and the other is bad to the bone – they know it and like it. Take a look to find out more about the different kinds of bad bosses and learn how to deal with a bad boss.

"Smothering Managers Are Bad News"

Dear Dave,

I work for a manager who is always breathing down our necks and feels she must oversee, touch, and control

everything and anything. We all feel she does not trust us and it is making us feel extremely uncomfortable and unproductive. The president of the company is always preaching about trusting us to do our jobs, but we sure don't feel like we can without being smothered. Please, give me some advice.

S

Dear S,

You are describing a real micro-manager at work. Micro-managing is when a manager cannot let go and trust people to do their work, so they manipulate, control, and over-manage even the smallest elements of an employees' work and the entire workplace. Instead of spending time doing their job training, developing, producing, and operating, they feel they must run and direct every detail.

Often, managers become this way because that is the way they were/are managed or, basically, they do not trust themselves, so how can they possibly trust others? It's a character flaw and managers who exhibit this behavior need education as well as a conscious decision to change from this poor management style.

What drives me crazy is we spend countless dollars on education, training, books, consultants, seminars, etc. on how to make managers better and trusting and allowing employees to do their jobs. However, the workforce is still laden with managers who would not trust their Mom if she said she loves them.

Empower, Not Devour

Managers must hire the right people, train them intensely, provide them clarity on goals and objectives, and then stand back to let the employees do their jobs. They should be around to guide employees and clarify and misunderstanding and confusion, but then – as one of my Rochester manager colleagues says – "Get the heck out of the way!"

Study after study shows that employees who feel they are trusted to do their jobs will do the jobs effectively and willingly. If they feel micro-managed or smothered, they will become sniveling pieces of molten flesh lying on the floor in a fetus position twitching like a toad.

So, the question is what can you do about your situation? You have choices and all of them are difficult and risky including:

You could confront the manager and tell her what you see and what is happening as a result of the micro-management situation. This can cause some problems as you know and, often, the messenger is shot.

You could consort with your fellow employees and send a clearly stated and factual letter to company executives, explaining the dilemma.

You could wait until your review – I hope you have one regularly – and tell your manager in very diplomatic ways about some ideas you have for increased productivity, which, of course, includes a more participative work environment where employees are empowered to do their job.

You can very diplomatically and sincerely ask company executives for education and training in management and leadership for present and prospective managers. This can be done as a positive gesture and a sincere interest in seeing the company personnel develop soundly.

Or, you can leave the company.

I, personally, believe that carefully thought-out and sincerely-expressed personal (one-on-one) communication with your manager about workplace issues is the best route. If you believe such confrontation would backfire and hurt your future at the company, then do not do it. However, if you think the manager may listen and really may want to improve, then a one-on-one dialogue may serve you well.

"Critical Boss Creates Unrest"

Dear Dave,

My boss is always looking for ways to pounce on me and my fellow employees. She is so critical and we are all on pins and needles. I have never heard her congratulate anyone for doing a good job. The only thing we hear is, "We better shape up or we are out." Why would a manager always be so critical? How can I cope with the way she treats us?

C

Dear C,

For starters, your boss believes that the best approach to management is being overly-critical and putting everyone on edge. I believe this kind of management causes more errors and problems to happen, because everyone is as jumpy as a frog in a fry pan.

My theory is that she probably was managed this way and it may be the only method she knows, or feels comfortable with. Managers tend to manage the way they were managed and her background is probably full of untrusting, command and control bosses, who spent a great deal of time looking for even the slightest mistakes, and then pounced on her.

You don't need to be a leadership genius to figure out that this type of management stifles the good contributions of the employees – everyone is busy practicing "CYA" techniques.

Coping With the Overly-Critical Boss

I believe that it would be extremely difficult to totally change your manager's behaviors and attitude. Her actions are a product of deeply-embedded beliefs and patterns of conduct. She has become skilled at creating this type of environment and, sadly, probably relishes the opportunities to practice her "critical craft."

However, I believe anyone can change and improve, but she will have to want to change the way she manages, or she will just resort back to these damaging behaviors at the drop of a hat. Sometimes, managers have to have monumental epiphanies that scare the pejeepers out of them in order to change, such as being fired for their misbehaviors.

I think your boss qualifies for Dave's "bosses from hell" nomination. But, even though you may not be able to change her, you can change the way you react to her attention to tension. I think you will find peace of mind by just working hard and not trying to fight her.

Communicate with her – Ask her how you can improve what you are doing and what things you should learn. Show her that you are eager to do great work and you want to become a more effective employee. This sends a strong signal that you only want to do what is best for the team and the company and it may keep her off of your back.

Be Professional. This is critically important. Always take the high road. Maintain a calm and professional demeanor in dealing with her, and don't let your emotions get out of hand. Take lots of deep breaths. Don't resort to name-calling or gossiping, but be straightforward and professional. If you bear the brunt of her attacks, listen, nod, provide results immediately, and move on.

Be analytical - Determine what issues are bugging her. Get her to prioritize what needs attention and always bring the conversation back to what you two can do together to move the team and company forward. Be proactive to take care of small problems before she pounces on you.

Finally, don't be hesitant to enlist the help of upper management or human resources if your boss remains continually abusive. If all else fails, move on.

"Good Managers Get Out of the Way"

Dear Dave,

Our "helicopter manager" cannot leave us alone and is smothering us to death. It is like she does not trust us to get busy and do our jobs. We are all dedicated workers and know what we are doing. Can you write something about this for all of those smothering managers out there?

T

Dear T,

Your letter reminds me of what management expert Peter Drucker said, "So much of what we call management consists in making it difficult for people to do their work."

Some managers need to learn is that, most of the time, the best thing they can do is get out of the way of the people actually doing the work. If you hired the right people, they are already motivated and will do their work properly.

Managers should spend more time focusing on the obstacles that may hinder people from doing their work by removing the barriers (lack of resources, knowledge, and goals) in front of the people doing the work, so that they can get busy.

Management writers suggest there are two reasons that make managers micromanagers:

Managers worry about being disconnected - As managers rise through the ranks, they often become concerned that they've lost touch with the actual work of the organization. Because they have less direct contact with the workers, or customers, they start to feel isolated.

Managers stay in familiar operational territory - Many managers are unable to let go of their old job, or their old ways of doing that job - they continue to spend time in the more comfortable operational realm of their employees.

Therefore, it is crucial that managers empower their people to manage day-to-day operations and be available to coach them as needed, rather than trying to do their work. In short, teach them, motivate them, and trust them.

Invasive management

I am sure we all have worked for a micromanager – I know I have - at some time during our careers. It is demoralizing. These control freaks are reluctant to delegate, second-guess everything we do, and no one learns anything.

Sadly, simple tasks that you could accomplish quickly, if left alone, take much longer. Your efforts may be thrown out as the micromanager completely re-does your work. Even worse, the micromanager may ridicule you and demean you in front of your peers – that really hurts.

In the world of "minimally invasive management," good managers have three primary jobs: they need to hire talented people; they need to train, develop, and serve their people; and they need to fire unproductive workers. That's management in a nutshell.

Your job

Understand - Start by understanding what causes your manager to act this way. Often it's a need for control that stems from insecurity - a lack of confidence that is exacerbated by a pressure to produce – both individually and as a team.

Show empathy - Remember, the micromanager is under pressure to hit goals. Show that you understand his or her struggles and are willing to share the load. This could be as simple as offering to help with additional tasks.

Speak up – prudently - Often micromanagers are oblivious to the impact they are having on other people. So, without being confrontational, find a way to let this person know how the "intense attention" is negatively affecting you and your team's productivity.

Shifting your boss's management style won't be easy, and it certainly won't be immediate. But if you can show her that you're trustworthy, thorough, and ultimately, on top of your work, you'll be able to inspire that change over time.

"Motivation Improves Morale"

Dear Dave

I am a manager at a large company. My fellow managers tend to lean on their employees and some even think it is good management to scare the crap out of their employees. I hope you can write some things about good motivation methods that managers will read in your column.

B

Dear B,

Simply, positive motivation builds positive morale. As a manager, your impact on employee motivation is immeasurable. By your words, your body language, and the expression on your face, you communicate your opinion of their value to the people you employ.

Feeling valued by their manager in the workplace is key to high employee motivation and positive morale. Feeling valued ranks right up there for most people with liking their work, good wages, opportunities for training and advancement, and feeling **in** on the latest news.

Building high employee motivation and morale is both challenging and yet somewhat simple. It requires that managers pay attention every day to meaningful aspects of employee well-being and be aware of their needs, fears, and desires.

Maximizing Management Motivation Momentum – That's a Mouthful!

Here is an inconvenient truth: how the manager appears and acts when they first arrive at work sets the tone for the day. I applaud managers that walk around the workplace and greet people. The opposite is the manager that arrives on the scene and suspiciously 'eyes' the employees like a Robin ready to pounce on a June bug.

Managers should also just use plain talk - use simple, yet powerful words to motivate employees How about please, thank you, and you're doing a good job (if they are). It is amazing how this courtesy and simple acknowledgement can elevate attitudes and behaviors. People want to know how they are doing, so tell them.

It is crucial for managers to let employees know what they expect. Not setting clear expectations is often a manager's first failure. Often, managers assume and think they have clearly stated work objectives, numbers needed, report deadlines, and requirements, but the employee received a different message and is not clear about what to do first.

Listen, we all know that business requirements change in the middle of the day, job, or project. This is an unavoidable fact. Managers must shift gears and employees must adapt and respond. But, while the new expectations are communicated - often poorly - the reason (the why) for the change, or the context for the change, is rarely discussed. This causes employees to think that the company leaders don't know what they are doing. Managers must explain the "why" things have changed and allow employees to help figure out "how" the change will happen.

Here's another gem for employee motivation and morale: Managers must make sure they get and appreciate feedback from the employee regarding what is going well and what needs improvement. Suffice it to say that the surest way to demotivate employees is to systematically shoot every messenger who bears vital information.

When I talk to other managers, the motivation and morale builder they identify most for themselves is knowing how they are doing at work. Employees need the same information.

They want to know – as soon as possible - when they have done a project well and when the manager is disappointed in their results.

Finally, managers must spend time daily with each employee. Managers should aim for an hour a week with each of their staff. Many studies indicate that a key employee work motivation factor is spending positive interaction time with the boss.

"Dealing With Management Isolation"

Dear Dave,

At my company, it seems like upper management has no clue about what is really going on. They seem to spend their time in isolation and do not get out on the floor to talk to their employees. I think they could learn a lot if they moved about the company more. What are your thoughts?

T

Dear T,

To be frank with you, *some* managers should isolate themselves. The reality is that some of us do have managers who may well be great at the technical parts of their work, but hopeless at their people management skills.

We have all had managers who keep their office door shut, barely finding time to even greet their staff each day. And then there are those managers who have their favorites, giving time to those they like and having little interaction with others.

Isolation causes stagnation. Stanford management professor, Robert Sutton warned against the "toxic tandem" of leadership, where managers become more self-absorbed and less attuned to others' perspectives, precisely when they need interaction and outside information the most.

Reasons for isolation

Managers need diverse opinions and ideas. There is an old saying: "One manger talks to his/her workers. Two managers talk to each other." This can lead to "seclusion delusion" where the manager receives information from a small number of people, who tend to think alike.

Appreciably, most managers have a heavy workload and are extremely busy. They work long hours and may spend a great deal of time interacting with people outside of the company. This precludes them from having more time to talk to their employees. This is a reason, not an excuse.

Managers are also often inundated with information - the volume of information top managers are able to process can be so great, they are literally overwhelmed. As a result, they have less time to listen to people and to gather and disseminate information.

The upper leadership isolation problem may also occur due to a common phenomenon that management writer, Ron Ashkenas, calls the "gatekeeping of senior executives." In many large organizations, executive assistants shelter their bosses to protect their limited time. This often leads to no time allotted to mingling with the workers.

Possible solutions for managers

When Jack Welch was CEO of GE, he created "listening posts," or meetings with managers from all parts of the company, where he could get truthful views and engage in more spontaneous dialogue. He then urged his managers to do the same by insisting that they lead "town meetings" with their employees.

Managers can also choose to set aside one hour every day - before anything consumes them - to concentrate on listening to employees. The goal is to make these discussion sessions routine, brief, and simple – but, mostly, to show employees they care about what they have to say.

The concept of "management by walking around" (MBWA) coined by management writers, Peters and Waterman exemplifies the art of mingling with employees. However, it involves more than walking around and listening: it involves being willing to listen to others, and by sharing information and responding to their new ideas.

Finally, managers, please open up your office door and let your employees know you are open for business. I know there are times when you must have the door closed, but, when you can, show employees you are approachable and willing to have conversations.

If you're in a leadership role, you can guard against being isolated by making connection and interaction a priority. Do it often and make it a routine priority.

"The Truth Shall Set You Free"

Dear Dave,

What happens when management does not tell the "whole truth" to employees, customers, and suppliers? Doesn't this send a signal to employees that it is OK to not be dishonest for the sake of making a profit?

Signed: B

Dear B,

You are correct. According to sites like "Bad Bossology," a lot of people work for men and women who would rather lie than tell the truth. It's hard work to lie - you have to keep track of your story and make sure details line up just right.

Managers as leaders set the tone and example - whether they know it or not - and employees are watching them to determine what is acceptable behavior and what is not. If management models dishonest practices, some employees will naturally follow the lead.

It all may start out as little lies or half-truths and escalate into a corporate condition where nothing can be believed. Managers must set the example and create a climate of truth and honesty. As brutal as honesty often can be, it would be worse to build hopes, or make business deals, based on lies and deception.

I believe some people tell lies because there is, sadly, a clear link between lying and success (temporary). We frustratingly see people getting away with small acts of deception to their advantage, but it is only short term. You will sleep better at night if you do not follow suit.

Why do People Lie?

Most of us embellish facts, or exaggerate in trivial ways - to make a story more interesting, or to gain sympathy from a friend, and the consequences are generally harmless. But, when bosses lie, the risk is great - low morale, a culture of deception, and even lost customers can all result.

Businesses are stressed and, often, have internal struggles going on. Upper management wants the most productivity for the least amount of payroll, and employees (most) want the most pay and satisfaction for the least amount of work, and things get said and done that are not totally 'above board', but there is never an excuse for dishonesty from either group.

If a manager needs to lie to make themselves look better and may be telling everyone what he or she thinks they want to hear, my belief is that you're working for an insecure leader. Your management is afraid of failing and they are afraid of making people angry, which is a paradox, because their actions tend to guarantee that result.

I'm sorry to say that I don't have a sure-fire way to confront a dishonest, insecure manager. But I do have a few tips that might help you and your co-workers out. The good news is that people in the position normally can't last too long. They'll lie to the wrong person, or shoot themselves in the foot, because they forgot what they said or did - you just don't want to go down with them.

Meet with a manager, who you feel will be sympathetic to your views. Be calm, businesslike, factual, and brief. Describe how the dishonesty is affecting the business (for example, low morale, low productivity, a high rate of calling in sick, or even theft).

Seek colleagues who behave ethically and form an alliance. I recommend meeting in a small group environment over multiple occasions to ensure participants' readiness to challenge the current system. Honesty finds strength in numbers – especially when folks consistently practice what they preach.

"Taking Over from an Incompetent Team Leader"

Dear Dave,

I have just been promoted to a great management position. Unfortunately, I am replacing someone who was a really bad and negative leader. This person was abusive and incompetent. My new employees don't really know me and they may even think I am just another bad manager. How can I get off on the right foot with them?

D

Dear D,

You say that "unfortunately" you are taking over for a bad leader. I say that the employees are fortunate to have the change in leadership. And, I respect your wish to do well and not repeat the mistakes of the past – that is a sign of true leadership.

Taking charge as the leader of an existing team can be challenging, but taking over from an incompetent leader is especially difficult. I advise you to, take your time and get to know the team - you'll get better results from your team if you invest the time to appreciate and respond to their needs and concerns and talk to them as valued team members.

By understanding what they have experienced, you'll better understand the issues that must be addressed to move forward - and your empathy will show your interest in your people's well-being, another thing that may have been lacking in the previous leader.

There are several other steps you can take:

Don't come in and change everything right away – Please don't blow everyone away with quick and possibly unclear assessments of what is right or wrong. Take some time to get a lay of the land and get the facts about the current environment and culture. You will gain more respect and trust if you take time to be a rational, patient leader, who analyzes things before acting.

Don't belittle the former boss – Badmouthing the former boss is not a smart tactic. Your purpose isn't to criticize the previous leader; it's to show the team that you have some understanding of the challenges they have faced and the effects it has had on the organization, the team, and them. Plus, badmouthing the former boss may make your team wonder what you might say about them.

Grasp what the team has experienced - If you know very little about what the team has been through, ask about the challenges they have faced and what fears and concerns they have. By clearly understanding what they have experienced, you'll develop a more complete picture of the existing climate and this will also demonstrate that you are interested in their well-being. Your goal is to build trust and confidence.

Get in the trenches with the team - Be a leader who models a great work ethic and is not afraid to dig in, work hard, and get things done. But, remember, your purpose is not to do their jobs, but to demonstrate the fact that you want results and realize it takes hard work to obtain them. Employees like leaders who model a strong work ethic and are action-oriented – not all talk.

Treat your people like valued individuals – Be sincere and sincerely interested in the well-being of your employees, their ideas, and their observations. Talk to them early and often. Offer help and any resources they may need. It is not a cardinal management sin to get close to your staff.

If you start off like a bull in a china shop, you will break a lot of china. Take time to understand, appreciate, and respond to your employees' needs and concerns before making changes. If you build relationships and show respect, respect will be given back to you.

"Managers Must Be Nice and Effective"

Dear Dave,

I have a problem. Our old boss was *not* a nice person, but seemed to know how to do the functional parts of her job. Our new boss is nice enough, but seems fairly incompetent. I

feel sorry for her, because she may be struggling and might be over her head. What can be done to help me and my team, and her?

S

Dear S,

Now, to be clear, both of these types of bosses are crappy (official leadership word) and having to choose between the two is sort of like deciding whether to be kicked in the stomach or kicked in the head.

I know having a nice boss is quite desirable, but I have seen so much damage done by lousy bosses who are really nice people in recent years that I am starting to wonder if a manager that is competent – but less than congenial - may be better.

Just know that incompetent bosses can seriously damage or derail your career. Also, if they do have a serious lack of knowledge and skills, they can do nothing to grow you as an employee, and can certainly never mentor you for future success.

What You Can Do

When you have an incompetent boss, you do have to think through and analyze how this person functions in order to use whatever strengths they do have to your advantage or, minimally, avoid career limiting outcomes. Let's look at some of the things you can do to prevail with an incompetent boss:

Understand the incompetence - Before you declare your boss totally useless, check your bias and better understand what you are seeing. Your assessment of her incompetence may be unfairly informed by these beliefs. But, of course, you may just discover you were absolutely right about her ineptness.

Leadership can come from you - If you know your job well, there is no reason to not go ahead creating and pursuing a direction you know will achieve results good for your company. People that do this are naturally followed by their peers as an informal leader, too.

Management, although maybe not your direct boss, will notice your initiative. But, be careful, you don't want to do something that undermines your boss, so keep her in the loop.

Be a teacher - Every time you speak to your boss you have an opportunity to train and teach her about you and your job. Also, instead of telling your boss what she should or should not do, phrase your statements in the form of suggestions. This way, you preserve her positional authority (she saves face) and plant the seeds of innovative ideas in your boss's mind.

Be an asset - Instead of approaching your boss as an obstacle to be dealt with, look at the relationship with an open, positive mindset. What might seem like shortcomings in your boss may actually be opportunities for you to be available and complement her management style.

Be forgiving –- Remember, this is a new relationship, so learn to look past first impressions, and give her the room and opportunity to grow. In the end, your giving her some grace will strengthen your new boss's commitment to you.

Often, you can make up for her short comings and also "manage up" as she probably knows that she lacks many skills and knowledge. Remember, you were new once and had a great deal to learn, so be of help – it will pay dividends.

"When the Leader is the Change Problem"

Dear Dave,

I have not seen my question in your column before: How do we get our manager to change when he is the problem in what we are trying to accomplish? Our manager means well, but he is not up to speed on how to really make things happen and lead people. We hear about the need to change all of the time, but our manager needs the change more than anyone.

M

Dear M,

Ooh … tough question and a sensitive one, too. The biggest obstacle is that, your manager probably thinks he is doing well, when the reality is otherwise. So, we have - in addition to the normal change struggles going on – the issue of pride and ego to contend with.

The truth is that, as leaders and problem solvers, our first strategies to bring about change will be to lock in on everything other than ourselves. So how do leaders fairly assess whether or not they are the change that needs to happen? And then, what do they do about it? This will take some truthful soul-searching.

I think we need to first realize that, just because someone holds a position of leadership, doesn't necessarily mean they should. The problem is, many organizations can't seem to recognize good leaders from bad ones and the bad ones often get promoted.

How leaders become the change problem

Managers need to hit goals and they must work through their people to meet them. This means they need to lead them. However, I believe leaders cannot lead others unless they can first lead themselves. This requires a thorough, honest, and fearless analysis by the leader to understand their strengths and weaknesses.

Effective leadership requires an ability to create and nurture change. Leaders must be change catalysts and get people on board with a change initiative. Even more fundamental is the motivation to change. Unless your manager can cope with these realities and needs, he will flounder and resist.

Listen, we all make mistakes, and there are some mistakes that managers make repeatedly. These include not giving good feedback, being too "hands-off," not delegating effectively, and misunderstanding one's role. Your manager may be lacking in all of these skills.

In addition, leaders must learn from their mistakes and help employees learn from theirs. But, if leaders don't take the time to understand their mistakes and how they impacted the people and the processes, they become even a bigger part of the problem.

How you can help

You can "manage your boss." Here are some strategies for you to use to approach him and help him become more effective. Your goal is not to belittle your manager, but to help him become a better leader. Remember, you may need to wait for the right opportunity to approach your boss.

First, discuss the specific problems amongst your team to determine if everyone sees and wants the same things. Then, compile a list of the things you need in order for whatever change you are working on to happen.

Then, go to your manager and kindly and gently – and objectively - ask for the resources and planning you need, and explain that you want to make sure you are doing things right. This will show your sense of purpose and will also help your manager feel like he is providing solutions.

Finally, support your manager and don't badmouth or him put down to co-workers. If you need to get input from other managers on dealing with your manager, focus on the goals and problems, not the person.

Chapter 4 – Effectiveness Must Be Effective

You've heard it said many times, "Garbage in, garbage out." In other words, if you work with lousy resources and do crappy work, crap is what you will get as a result. Effective organizations create results, and to be fully effective, they must exhibit strengths in five core organizational areas—leadership, decision making and structure, people, work processes and systems, and culture.

Even though the quality movement has been going on for scores of years, we, at work, still cut corners in projects and tasks, and use less than the best methods we can find or already possess. Now, you could create a laundry list of why this is so, but I think the biggest reasons are a lack of time and a lack of attention.

I think about these things most when I am sitting on a plane ready for takeoff. I hope and pray that there are hundreds of skilled, dedicated, Type A, OCD workers who fastidiously checked every nut and bolt on the plane with a lighted microscope just before I got on. I hope that the pilots got a great night's sleep and have been exercising and eating right to be on top of their game. And I hope the people in the control tower are spending an inordinate amount of time watching and guiding the plane to a special, secluded runway that was just freshly paved.

However, this is not reality and people make mistakes. The biggest problem is when people know they could prevent a mistake and choose to do nothing. These folks are not proactive and they are not even reactive in their selected neglect. That's when everything in the company falls apart and errors are as common as ants at a picnic.

What can we do to increase the effectiveness at work? One thing we can do is hire the best people we can find – it's amazing what that will do for quality. Another things is for management to settle for nothing less than optimal performance and output. This requires training, education, abundant resources and use of the best systems and methods available. Please read on to find out what else it may take for quality and effectiveness to happen at work.

"Easy May Not Be Best"

Why do people always take the easy way out of situations? When my fellow managers and I meet to try and solve problems, we always seem to find answers that

are easy to use, but may not be the best answers to really take care of things.

R

Dear R,

I don't believe people look for the hard way to do things, but, in reality, difficult challenges may require difficult questions, answers, and responses.

We should not, however, seek the hardest way to do things. We should seek effective solutions that are the least difficult to understand, buy-into, and implement. It would be nonsense to complicate things, simply because we may believe there are no 'simple' solutions. Often there are.

Fundamentally, efficiency (often fast, cheap, and easy) does not *always* equate to effectiveness (whole solutions). But, we live in an age that thrives on and covets speed, and we become victims of quick closure at any cost – which often means fast responses that do not fully take care of things.

Good is Not Great

Efficiency is doing things right, but effectiveness is doing the right things. In short, when you implement a new solution, it is likely to make things more efficient. However, if you do not properly align the people, processes, resources, and technology, you are unlikely to make your business more effective.

A company should seize the opportunity to 'fully' examine and redesign their business processes to make sure they are both efficient and effective, given the new and projected demands of any company in a very turbulent economic environment.

The battle cry of 'doing more with less' has also had great impact, because funds have dried up and headcounts have shrunk. This has caused companies to seek quick solutions that are passable, but not always optimal. Excellence must be excellent.

To make things worse, this need for speed and quick solutions – versus best responses – becomes part of the culture and may even be rewarded by management. There becomes a fondness and admiration for 'any answers in a hurry'. This may even mean that careful planning gives way to pace and appropriate actions give way to 'do whatever you think'.

Measuring Effectiveness

So, how does a company determine whether they are truly operating effectively? According to one of my Rochester management colleagues, who hates sloppy decisions and actions, there are several key indicators that, if not addressed, could be damaging to a business' health, image, and bottom line:

Customer service: A high number of complaints, or overall poor customer satisfaction

Compliance: Difficulty in meeting filing procedural requirements and agreements

Budget disasters: Consistently missing budget

Cost containment: Difficulty in minimizing costs and remaining competitive

Turnover: High unplanned turnover

What to Do

As a manager, you should examine your current processes to help to eliminate non-value added activities and identify opportunities to redesign and streamline the processes. Try to convince your management colleagues that changes in the organizational structure may strengthen efficiency and effectiveness and result in the ability to fully solving problems.

Explain to others that if things are not fully taken care of, the problems will re-emerge and may be more devastating later. Sell the fact that nagging problems may require challenging responses, but the end result is well worth the costs.

When you meet, ask the tough questions that may make people uneasy about fully solving problems, or to exploit opportunities. You will need to model a mission of correctness and completion. You may not always make friends, but you may help the company survive and prosper.

"Behavior That Promotes Positive Change"

Dear Dave,

My company struggles with any form of change. I know people resist change for many reasons, but our management does not seem to understand what it takes to change the thinking. What can managers do to promote positive change in the workplace?

T

Dear T,

I believe managers can foster positive change through understanding organizational behavior, which is crucial to success in business. Defined, organizational behavior is any type of behavior resulting from the structure and culture of the organization.

Managers can influence organizational behavior and nurture positive change by increasing the competence and confidence of staff. For instance, training that show employees how to solve problems within the organization is one way to improve their performance.

I'm not suggesting that managers treat employees like rats in a maze; I am only indicating that, usually there are inhibitors of change and managers must find out what they are, and find ways to address the inhibitors. In short, decrease the bad (resistance and obstacles) and increase the good (tools and motivation).

Let me clarify that resistance is not always a bad sign. Some resistance happens because the change(s) just doesn't make sense, or is not well-thought-out. In these cases, resistance means people are thinking and trying to sort things out.

Increase the Good

Rather than chastise and condemn, it is far better for managers to encourage and support. Here are some tools and ideas:

Collaborative Planning - One of my Rochester management colleagues tells me, organizations need to plan for change by minimizing risk and maximizing return. To do this requires input and ideas from all employees.

Accordingly, managers must identify barriers to positive change in the workplace, so they can eliminate potential obstacles from the outset. For instance, surfacing change biases is crucial and employees must identify their own biases about change, which can eliminate misunderstanding by opening up communication.

Continuous Feedback - Most companies and organizations use an evaluation system to ensure that workers are meeting necessary job standards. However, having a yearly evaluation does little to foster ongoing positive change.

Instead, having a positive feedback system in place will result in greater motivation and change. Employees who are trained to focus on the positive aspects of their own behavior will think and focus on positive change, rather than thinking only about what they are doing wrong.

Promote Team Thinking - In every organization collective knowledge is important. Group thinking is important, because workers feel they are united by a common purpose. Plus, when employees increase their participation levels, change buy-in goes up.

Workers united by a common identity and purpose must be reminded by management of this shared identity on a regular basis. In addition, workers who share a common identity and purpose will be more likely to unite and implement positive change.

Evaluating Change - Organizations can also measure change in a number of different ways. For instance, companies can create surveys that measure the willingness of employees to change certain behaviors or organizational practices.

In the same vein, the effectiveness of that change can be measured by evaluating the opinions and perceptions of employees once changes have been implemented.

Employees have many concerns about change – mostly, because they feel that change happens 'to them' and not 'with them'. Employee behaviors promoting change will only happen if the change makes sense, employees see personal value in the change, and if employees feel like they have ownership (through participation) in the change.

"Look at the Pieces and the Whole"

Dear Dave,

At my company, we are encouraged to find and take care of big problems. What drives me nuts are the small, nagging problems. I know that, taking care of big things is important, but how can I, my manager, and my coworkers start focusing on the small things, too.

R

Dear R,

I believe big problems are usually a system and conglomeration of numerous small problems. For example, a company may find that their most talented employees are leaving the company at a fast pace and, when breaking that problem down in to 'bite-size' pieces, managers find many factors, such as lack of growth opportunities, lack of motivation, or even dislike for certain managers.

So … we can identify the big problem, but we really need to take care of the elements contributing to the big problem, either one-by-one or simultaneously. This calls for a factor analysis of sorts and everything related to the main problem - large or small – must be put on the table for evaluation.

I'm reminded of the saying, "A chain is only as strong as its weakest link." Accordingly, every 'link' in the problem chain must be checked for strength and functionality. I guess what I am saying – stay with me here – the organization must sell the idea to employees of looking both at the whole and the pieces at the same time.

Looking at the Whole

A doctor does not look at one aspect of our health in isolation; rather he or she looks at the entirety of our physical – and possibly – mental state of affairs. The doctor knows that one aspect 'out of whack' (not a medical term) can derail our general health.

That's why we continuously hear our doctors telling us to eat right, exercise, and lose some weight – at least I do. These are individual problems and challenges that, if addressed, will improve my general health.

In the same fashion, an organization's health is dependent on how we take care of the various pieces. An honest and searching assessment of the organization will result in the revelation of many health issues, including big things like cultural and quality problems, or smaller, aggravating things – to your point – like running out of supplies, people not responding to messages, or even ineffective meetings.

Selling this Concept to Everyone

As my wife always tells me, "Look beyond the end of your nose." With this in mind, we need to keep our eyes open to "look at the house and the individual rooms" at the same time. This is a way of thinking and managers must model, support, and teach this type of thinking.

We are surrounded by systems, not convenient, straight, linear paths of cause and effect. We need to look at the impact of one thing on another and how adjusting – or not adjusting – one thing may totally disable or enhance something else.

For instance, the failure of a high school student may not be due to lack of study; it may be because of the stresses a student is experiencing, or even a lack of family support. At work, the dysfunctional nature of an employee may not be due to a 'bad attitude'; rather, it could involve many things such as antagonistic coworkers, a lack of job skills, or fear and insecurity.

Managers set the example. If employees see managers thinking systemically, they may also do the same. If they see managers solving those 'nagging small problems' quickly and completely, and not just be on a march to save the universe, they, too, may follow suit. It then becomes "the way things are done."

"If You Fail To Plan, Then Plan to Fail"

Dear Dave

I started working for an organization in Rochester about 6 months ago. What I've noticed is something I am not used to – management knows how to write good plans, but they do a lousy job of executing them. It's such a waste, because we spend so much time collecting information and planning. Any ideas?

R

Dear R,

I'm reminded of the saying, "If you fail to plan, then plan to fail," but in your case, it's more like, "If you fail to execute the plan, then plan to be executed." However, I know exactly what you mean and I have seen this problem before.

I am amazed at why managers would not implement a plan that they have spent so much time on. They have spent time gathering data. They have taken the data and analyzed it. They have planned from the facts they have uncovered. Then, they very expeditiously put the plan on the shelf and every-so-often glance at it and say, "There it is – one heck of a plan!"

One study reveals that each year the average organization spends 20,000 person hours on planning, budgeting, and forecasting for every $100 million in annual revenue. With an investment of this magnitude, it makes sense that most companies would run their plans.

Executing the Execution

The strategic planning process in most organizations, if there even is a process in place, can be flawed. The planning process in many companies consists of executive retreats each year, wherein the senior management of the organization discuss planning and where they want to take the business.

The output of this process is often a plan document full of ideas with some goals, objectives, and milestones. Unfortunately, in many cases, that's where the planning process for that year often ends.

Why do most plans go unexecuted? Is it simply human nature, or are there other demonic forces at work here? The lack of execution typically has a lot to do with the lack of a system, structure, and flow for actual plan execution. The firm, Project Leadership Associates came up with 5 barriers to executing a plan:

1. The underlying plan strategy is not clear - Many companies have unclear basic organizational strategies. This leads to confusion, ranging from "fuzziness" in direction, to silent conflict among staff, to a breakdown of understanding among managers and employees.

2. The plan is overly optimistic - Runaway optimism builds failure into the plan, corrupting the entire notion of execution in the minds of the people required to follow through and in the processes required to maintain the 'realistic' plan outcomes.

3. No one is accountable for results - Accountability is the unseen force that motivates individuals to follow through on their commitments. A primary driver of accountability is clarity on "who is on the hook for what."

4. The plan has not been actively deployed - At first hearing, most employees will not understand a plan enough to apply it to their activities and responsibilities. At worst, the result is mismatched expectations regarding what management has actually committed to.

5. The plan is static - Within many of the plans that end up in overstuffed binders locked away in the credenza, there is an unspoken assumption that nothing happening either inside or outside of the company can change the validity of the plan. Wrong!

Successful plan execution is a living, dynamic process. That's why it is important to distinguish between planning and execution — an ongoing process for reviewing and maintaining progress.

"If You Meet, Then Make Decisions"

Dear Dave:

At my company, our meetings are a joke and seem to accomplish nothing. We always push things into the next meeting. What do good business decision-makers do when trying to solve problems and do it quickly?

T

Dear T,

Meetings should be serious business, but rarely start on time, address core issues (that should be discussed), and involve the higher-level thinking necessary for in-depth analysis and decision-making.

What often results at meetings is a lot of bias and embedded beliefs, lower-level pro and con discussion, and tabling – until the next ineffective meeting – the dialogue and solutions that should be, or could be, made at the current meeting.

Granted, many companies and organizations do a better job of conducting meetings and making necessary decisions than others. However, many think they are doing a good job of making decisions, when all they are really doing is passing blame, arguing by prejudice, and avoiding making definitive and implementable decisions.

Decision-Making Help 101

Your decision to learn about better decision making is a good decision. First, it is imperative that everyone involved in a decision-making process truly define the core problem(s) that exist and come to agreement that the 'problem' really is the problem that exists.

Try this simple 5-step model recommended by business-analysis-made-easy.com:

1. Analyze the facts, data, and information available.

2. Define alternative solutions.

3. Discuss the alternatives thoroughly for merit, impact, or weaknesses.

4. Pinpoint the absolute best solution.

5. Implement it.

I will add two more things to this decision-making model: Measure and monitor your solution; and adjust your solution as needed. Thus, the decision-making process becomes a system of analysis, development, score-keeping, and continuous improvement.

Fatal Errors to Avoid

One of my Rochester management colleagues suggests that valid data and information should drive the decisions, not unwarranted assumptions or biased hunches. This requires all decision makers to be brutally honest in learning the facts and not what they only think they are.

Unfortunately, people make repetitive, common errors in decision making that impede the quality and caliber of the decisions. Here are a few bad practices noted by management writer, Richard Daft:

1. Using shortcuts: This is giving up the "right way" to do things in favor of, 'get there, but get there fast and the easiest way'. Efficiency is not always effectiveness!

2. Satisficing: This is lowering your standards often forsaking quality or excellence, and good enough is viewed as excellent.

3. Using Rules of thumb: This is using only best guesses and not getting all of the necessary information for making good decisions.

Again, you cannot find the right solution if you cannot even state the real problem. Get the data. Look at reports. Find out what your customers and employees think. Think about what have you heard that should be checked out? What feedback do you have from various stakeholders about what is working and what is not? Get a clear picture of 'what really is' going on.

Put everything out in front of you on the table, so everyone can see what the factors are and what and whom is having impact on the problem, or being impacted by the problem. This is called transparency – the truth drives the decisions.

Finally, and all too often, people analyze things to death and then do nothing. Management guru, Peter Drucker stated, "The death of any good solution is inaction." This means, sooner or later, you need to pull the trigger and fully implement the decision.

"Ideas Are Easy; Execution Is Hard"

Dear Dave,

At my company we have no shortage of ideas, but we lack the ability to take action on things we create. How can we best take ideas to implementation, so we can get things done? I don't think we have hit a deadline in years – but we brainstorm like experts.

K

Dear K,

I think most people like the creative part of thinking up new ideas, but lose their ambition and desire when confronted with the task of executing the ideas. However, thankfully, there are workers who will make the "rubber meet the road" and will take things to the launch phase and ensure execution happens according to plans. We need more of these people!

I also think one of most frustrating challenges facing leaders today is closing what is known as the "execution gap." The execution gap is a perceived gap between a company's expectations and its ability to meet those goals and put ideas into action. We realize companies must be innovative, but innovation assumes that the creative ideas actually become implemented and measured.

Because companies operate in a complex, chaotic, and uncertain world, pulling the trigger on plan execution is often difficult for leaders. One recent survey found that 49% of business leaders perceived a gap between strategy and execution and 64% lacked confidence in their company's ability to close the gap.

Why some people and teams can't bring well-designed plans to the action phases could fill volumes. But, generally, the reasons include a lack of implementation know-how, a lack of resources, and unclear expectations, goals, and roles. To make things worse, plan execution is perceived as a threat, because it means that ideas and designs will actually be tested – people don't want to look bad if plans fail.

What to do

Even though execution is difficult, managers have the responsibility of getting things done. They must tune into the people, processes, and parts that make up the execution piece of planning. Here are some ideas for closing the execution gap.

Clearly define the most desired end result – Ideas and initiatives need a clearly defined purpose, a vision, and goals. Unclear definitions will lead to a lack of employee buy-in and will produce lousy results. The more specifically you can define your ideas, expectations, and deliverables, the more employees will know what they're supposed to be working toward.

Clearly articulate the "Why" – Make sure you effectively communicate to your employees what is supposed to be done and, more importantly, why they should be doing it. Clearly and concisely communicate the value of initiatives and what they will mean to employees on a personal and team level.

Acquire the necessary resources and knowledge - To make sure strategies get put into motion, you must make sure you have the knowledge, skills, and resources to manage the project. You can't expect people to execute effectively if they don't have the know-how and tools.

Allow your employees to be rational skeptics – Get all of the risks, assumptions, fears, and denial on the table. If people can view the impact of actions and are able to openly question the ideas and conduct respectful debate and deliberation, the more you can reduce the fears that will prevent effective execution.

Celebrate incremental achievements - Breaking down a long execution process into "bite-sized" pieces, and celebrating each milestone as they are reached, is a practice that allows leaders to acknowledge and recognize the hard-won accomplishments their teams are making.

Today's fiercely competitive marketplace requires us all to take rhetoric to reality. A great plan or idea that is not executed responsibly and thoroughly achieves nothing.

"Embrace Constructive Conflict"

Dear Dave,

My team gets into a lot of heated debates with each other. They are all good people and good workers, but their opinions tend to dominate their thinking. I don't want people at each other's throats, but I do like the fact that my employees feel strongly about things and want to improve things. How can I handle this?

P

Dear P,

I was taught in graduate charm school that consensus is overrated and people must express their views and try to come up with the best solutions, not just agree to agree. A rush to judgment usually brings less-than-effective ideas and measures to really solve problems and exploit opportunities.

Finding the right balance between the need to deal with conflict and the instinct to avoid it is one of the toughest challenges that managers face. While uncontrolled conflict can create a toxic atmosphere, insufficient conflict can be just as damaging, because creative ideas and better ways of getting things done – which help organizations advance – often stem from constructive conflict.

Conflict as a friend

You can encourage constructive conflict by reinforcing the notion that people can disagree about ideas and strategies, practices, and processes, but still respect and are kind to each other. I think everyone likes the idea of being challenged – though, some may not appear that way – so stir up the pot and challenge people to think.

There must be a shift in mindset that creative ideas and better ways of getting things done often stem from constructive conflict. I believe companies are full of bright, ambitious people with different points of view, controversial ideas, and creative perspectives. The trick is to hear what they have to say and encourage them to take thoughts and ideas to action and implementation.

It's important to remind your employees that no one person is perfect and always right. Doing this will reinforce the notion that employees can disagree with each other about ideas and strategies, but still respect and like each other. Teach employees how to ask better questions and not instantly have "knee jerk" solutions for everything.

Also, try to schedule times with your team to question the way things are done and surface ideas for improvement. Create open idea forums that provide employees the opportunity to share what they are thinking and to safely challenge those who may be inclined to keep doing things the same old unproductive way. Make it clear that the messenger will not be shot and the forums are places that are "safe for thinking." This also allows people who might hesitate to raise issues by themselves feel more comfortable doing so in a group.

Recognize employees who constructively question the status quo - give them positive reinforcement. If someone pushes back or raises an uncomfortable question in a meeting, explore what they have to say, rather than shutting them down. Make questions and idea sharing an opportunity to learn how to be more innovative.

Finally, set ground rules for conflict. Since everyone struggles with conflict to some degree, develop a few standards for how your team can manage it constructively. Guidelines for debate will help nurture collaborative thinking and help people keep a grip on their emotions. Shouting matches turn people off, make them defensive, and polarize their thinking.

In summary, nothing good comes out of stale paradigms of thinking. It takes some debate and positioning to shake things up and then collectively come up with some great, new ideas. The key is to ensure everyone plays nice, does not take things personal, and works together to think at higher levels.

"Job Descriptions are Mandatory"

Dear Dave,

Since joining my company, I have been asking for a job description and exactly what my performance goals are. I probably should have asked for all of this before I started my job, but I was so happy to finally get a job I did not want to seem real picky. Any thoughts on this?

M

Dear M,

Good, descriptive, and specific performance expectations come from well-written job descriptions. You have a double whammy problem in that you have neither one. An employee can hardly be effective if they do not know exactly what their job is and how they will be evaluated.

A lack of clear performance expectations is usually chosen by employees as a key contributing factor to their happiness or unhappiness at work. In fact, in a recent poll about what makes a bad boss bad, the majority of respondents said that their manager did not provide clear direction.

Taking the time to set and communicate clear expectations can help eliminate many performance problems. Setting performance expectations helps focus on the goals and objectives, as well as prioritize duties that are significant to accomplishing those objectives.

Jobs and Expectations

A job description describes the major areas of an employee's job and includes information about the tasks involved, the methods used to complete the tasks, the purpose and responsibilities of the job, the relationship of the job to other jobs, and the qualifications needed for the job.

Managers can make a job description practical by keeping it specific, functional, understandable, and current. A Rochester HR specialist tells me, well-written, practical job description will help a manager avoid having employees refuse to carry out a relevant assignments, because it isn't 'in their job description'.

In short, job descriptions provide standards that can be used to judge employee performance. This provides the foundation for employee compensation programs and for comparing the relative worth of each job's contributions to the company's overall performance.

Goals of Employee Performance Evaluation

These are the goals of an effective employee evaluation process:

The employee and the manager are clear about the employee's goals, required outcomes or outputs, and how the success of the contributions will be assessed.

The goals of the best employee performance evaluations are also employee development and organizational improvement.

Employee performance evaluation provides legal, ethical, and visible evidence that employees were actively involved in understanding the requirements of their jobs and their performance.

For You

It is a best practice in employment – for both your manager and you - to have up to date job descriptions. Reasons for this include clarification of what exactly your job entails and from your employer's point of view makes it easier to appraise you, identify training requirements, and most importantly, let you know how you are doing.

Because of the recession, employees have taken on more responsibilities and duties which means that some managers - maybe yours - thinks job descriptions may be hard to write. However, you do have a legal right to have with a written statement of the main terms and conditions of your employment, which should include a thorough explanation of your job functions and how you will be held accountable.

I would suggest that you approach your manager and ask for your job description to be updated and clarified. You could offer to prepare a job description based on the role that you have been doing since you started, which can then be amended by agreement.

"Take Care of Your Customers and Employees"

Quote of the Day: "The world is so dreadfully managed, one hardly knows to whom to complain."

Ronald Firbank

Dear Dave,

I know managers should make employees happy and rewarded and all of the other stuff that you and other writers say, but work is work, it's competitive as heck, and things just need to get done. Don't you think my employees' motivation should be trying to keep their job? You probably won't use my question

M

Dear M,

No, I will use your question and I will try to stay calm. My first thought is, employees are people with emotions, thoughts, and feelings – not to forget ideas and creativity - and they should be treated as such. If you want robots, contact one of those robotic manufacturing companies.

From what I can tell, you sound like a hard worker and expect others to work hard, too. That is a good thing and hard work often gets things done. Also, I agree with you that workers who have work should be grateful. Finally, in these tough times, any organization realizes what you realize and the fact is survival rests on out-selling, out-servicing, and just plain beating their competition.

Organizations want results and results can mean different things to different people. A simple explanation is that results are produced when an organization is motivated and applies processes and resources to achieve targeted goals. However, results only tell a part of the story and - just like you - employees crave and need respect, appreciation, recognition, and rewards.

I tell my Augsburg MBA students there are two groups you need to satisfy each and every day - your customers and your employees. Without fulfilled and satisfied customers, your doors will be closed, and without fulfilled and dedicated employees, no customer will ever be completely satisfied.

Dave's Success Equation:

Happy Employees + Happy Customers = Happy Profitable Company

Therefore, management - as I always try to explain and teach in my rants and diatribes - requires more than accountability and pressure, and necessitates those nasty little employee management nuisances like instilling trust, delegating responsibly, empowering people, inspiring them to contribute and feel they are part of a great thing, and helping them become the best they can be.

Trust Dave on this one: if you make your employees satisfied and fulfilled, they will work wonders for you. In short, they will do the required work and also perform the value-added things that produce customer satisfaction.

Grow your people

You need to think in terms of succession and who will be ready and capable to assume and be effective in vacant leadership positions. This will only happen if you challenge and motivate people, so they can become the best they can be. If all you have are cowering, nervous wrecks, who are fearful for their jobs, you will have zip, nada, zero willing and able future leaders.

Employees want growth opportunities, a chance to do their best work and maximize the use of their skills, and they want to be able to work without smothering, intimidating managers breathing down their necks. Yes, they want job security, but they also want organizational "social security" where they feel good about their management and colleague relationships and bonds.

A company is primarily made up of people, processes, strategy, information, structure, and rewards. If any of these pieces is absent, all kinds of crazy things start happening, not least of which is good people saying good-bye and going elsewhere. Take care of your people and let them achieve and grow. And, make sure they are rewarded fairly and often, beyond just keeping their job.

"Potential Improvements Are Everywhere"

Dear Dave,

At my company, all employees are expected to constantly look for ways to improve things. As a manager, I am having difficulty getting my employees to buy into the idea – it seems like everyone is so locked into the way they do things, they do not want to change. Any ideas?

D

Dear D,

I hear you, loud and clear. Businesses need to be innovative and must constantly be on the prowl to improve the things they offer and do. But, innovation means the 'C word' (change) and that word sends terror into the hearts and minds of many.

I assume your management is looking for ways to cut costs, while improving efficiency and effectiveness. This underscores the assumption that anything can be improved –

something I whole-heartedly believe in. However, we know human nature, and the worrying about the past and agonizing about the future inhibits our ability to think in the now.

Inhibitors of Innovation

Your problem could be a management problem. One of my Rochester management colleagues tells me, many managers claim to understand the importance of innovation, but in reality, they desperately fear it, since innovation means to do what has not been done.

That's why most managers find it is easier and certainly safer to do what they have always done -recognizing and embracing innovation is a risk, but not nearly so much as rejecting it.

Ron Ashkenas (HBR Blog) describes some common inhibitors to an organization's ability to innovate effectively. Think about the extent to which these apply to your firm:

Our focus on short-term results drives out ideas that take longer to mature.

Most of our resources are devoted to day-to-day business, so that few remain for innovative prospects.

Innovation is someone else's job and not part of everyone's responsibilities.

We do not have a standard process to nurture the development of new ideas.

Managers are not trained to be innovation leaders.

Managers immediately look for flaws in new ideas, rather than consider their potential.

We look at opportunities through internal lenses, rather than starting with customers' needs and problems.

What You Can Do

Those with an innovative mind-set operate in the present, but plan for the future. For them, their contentment is their discontent with what has not been done or could be done. Consider these suggestions.

Share the entrepreneurial vision – the vision must be permeated throughout the organization in order for your employees to understand the company's direction and share in the responsibility for growth.

Increase awareness of opportunities – take time to show your employees the value of what they do and how their roles contribute to what the company does. The awareness of their functionality can increase the recognition of possibilities.

Sell the concept of change – increase a preference for change versus hanging on to the status quo. However, provide ample resources for change and reduce the obstacles preventing change.

Sell the desire to be innovative – create an environment that allows 'reasonable' risk and experimentation. Allow failure to be a learning experience and reward attempts at innovation.

Listen to your employees and be flexible – how you model a willingness to accept and even implement innovative ideas will dictate the willingness of your employees to offer innovative ideas. How you innovate determines what you innovate.

Create a sense of urgency – employees must recognize the fact that innovation is the imperative to the organization's competitiveness and sustainability. "Innovate or Die!"

"Never Give Up"

Dear Dave,

It seems like my colleagues give up on things way too easily. They throw in the towel before giving a project or change their best shot. Everything gets tabled or just squashed. Why would people give up on things so easily and what can be done about it?

R

Dear R,

Winston Churchill said, "Never give up on anything you can't go a day without thinking about." We start off with the best of intentions, but we also start off projects and tasks with some pessimism, skepticism, and fear. The problem is, we often let even the smallest obstacles derail us, because we believe they are much more adverse than they really are.

Work can be tough – it can make us masters of avoiding starting or completing it. Remember that the times when it's most important to persevere are the times that you will be most tested.

More on why people give up

I think the biggest reason people give up is, because they only look at how far they have to go, instead of how far they have gotten. We should be proud of what have accomplished, and not be discouraged or overwhelmed by what we still have to do. We simply cannot let the distance between where we are and where we need to be scare the pejeepers out of us.

Some would say that we may just become complacent, even lazy, and our initial energy and passion has waned to the point where we start doubting ourselves and even think, "Why in the heck did we even embark on this mission?" Then, collective doubting kicks in and all you start hearing is reasons why this or that cannot be accomplished, and not why they can.

Research shows that the attraction for whatever we hope to do, have, or become is a far less powerful motivating force than our desire to avoid the inevitable pain we experience while we're trying to achieve them. Simply, pain avoidance is more powerful than pleasure fulfillment.

Another reason we get discouraged and quit too early is we set our expectations too darn high to begin with. Setting aggressive, but reasonable and doable goals will help keep our energy and momentum going, while building our confidence to hit them.

Staying Motivated

So how do you stay motivated and on track with your goal? Here's what you can do:

Think "why" - When I get discouraged I just think about my "Why" and the reason I am doing what I'm doing. Thinking about my "Why" gives me purpose and motivation.

Know your goals - The larger the goals, the more work it takes to get hit them. Break up the goals into "bite-sized" and measurable action items that, if met, will fulfill the larger goals. And, make sure you obtain the resources you need to complete the work.

Assign roles and accountabilities - Make sure everyone knows their responsibilities and how what they do will be measured. Then, motivate each other by keeping a positive attitude and praising work well done.

Incremental rewards - Take the time to celebrate your small successes, your insights, and discoveries, not just the end result. As one of my Rochester management colleagues says, "What gets rewarded, gets repeated."

In conclusion, please understand that some pursuits are an actual waste of time and resources. There are times when you should thrown in the towel. So, set up realistic measures, so you know exactly when it may be time to give up. However, don't set easily-attainable goals that do not produce anything.

Chapter 5 – They Call It Leadership

So much is written about leadership, yet, we have a hard time defining it. However, we know it when we see it … and when we don't and should. Most people would agree that great leaders have strong, well-developed traits. I believe leadership happens when the right people do the right things at the right time. Sorry, I know that sounds fluffy, but, I believe situations and timing test people and the best leaders actually do something right by taking care of the business at hand. Person meets moment and leads people.

On the other hand, Leadership is inherent in the very nature of the organization. It arises from the peculiar relationships and bonds that form among people joined together in a purpose-driven collaborative effort. As such, it takes on an identity of its own, existing in these relationships, rather than merely in the individuals who enter into them. This is termed the culture of the organization and leaders know that, if they don't understand the culture, they will not know how to lead the organization Thus, leadership both influences, and is influenced by, those tightly-knit groups of individuals.

Let's also talk about what leadership is *not*... Leadership is not seniority or one's position in a company. Leadership doesn't automatically happen when you reach a certain management level – you need to develop it and apply it. To be clear, leadership has nothing to do with titles. I stress the fact that you don't need a title to lead. In fact, you can be a leader anywhere without a title.

It's also true that leadership has nothing to do with personal attributes. We don't need extroverted charismatic traits to practice leadership. And those with vivacious personalities and charisma don't automatically lead like George Washington. Finally, leadership isn't management – please get that straight. We know managers need to plan, organize, coordinate, solve, hire, fire, and so many other things. Typically, managers manage *things*. Leaders lead people.

To be sure, in an intelligently managed organization, that leadership isn't a randomly operating process; it's a strong, thrusting force given motion by purpose, commitment, desire, and by a joint effort to accomplish it. But it is management's role to ensure that this organizational leadership has a substantive and meaningful core around which to form itself and to give it traction and momentum for advancing the organization toward its most desired state.

Leadership is more often than not about "soft skills" rather than hard skills. Yes, a leader who understands what drives the bottom line is valuable. Yet it's the leader who can get *others* to perform at their best who ultimately creates winning organizations. To do this leaders use ethical persuasion and they just, plain talk to their people heart-to-heart.

Organizational leadership is more than just management – it is about understanding how human behavior influences a company's success, and how individuals can harness the strengths and expertise of a group's workers to maximize effectiveness. Corporate culture, group dynamics and strategic planning are all key elements of organizational leadership, and aspiring business leaders can learn these principles.

"The Best Leaders Are both Tough and Nice"

Dear Dave,

I have asked other managers in my company about the best ways to lead my employees. I hear some managers say that it is best to be tough and demanding, while other managers say I should be nice, friendly, and caring. These views seem conflicting. What do you think?

T

Dear T,

Every leader wonders whether it's best to be tough or nice. I don't believe it is an "or" question, but, rather an "and" question – an artful and thoughtful blend of both approaches is best for leaders. You can and should be relationship-oriented, while being appropriately demanding of results.

Nice is the ability to nurture, coach, inspire, respect, and truly care for those you lead. Tough is driving hard for success, pushing plans and measurement, setting lofty goals, holding people accountable, and making the tough decisions. These approaches are not opposites - they are compatible.

However, different situations and different people may require varying levels of the two approaches. But, I believe almost every employee understands there are demands and expectations they must meet, and that they desire to do so under leaders that treat them with respect.

Drivers and Enhancers

Leadership writers, Zenger and Folkman, believe leaders often use one of two styles: "Drivers" are good at establishing high standards, keeping people focused on goals, and continuous improvement. "Enhancers," by contrast, act as role models, give honest feedback in a helpful way, develop people, and maintain trust.

These management writers also claim that neither approach on its own is sufficient to increase employee engagement. Instead, they ask managers to mesh the two approaches as needed – a manager can demand a great deal from employees, but also be seen as considerate, trusting, approachable, and collaborative.

If you're tough - a "Driver" - you can push people to maximize their abilities. If you're nice - an "Enhancer" - you can better understand the needs, problems, and concerns of your staff. So, which style results in the more highly-engaged employees?

Survey Says

According to a study of 160,576 employees working for 30,661 managers, the tough-versus-nice debate is close. Eight percent of tough-led employees are highly engaged versus six percent of the nice-led employees. However, the most effective leaders, it turns out, mesh both styles, and 68 percent of their employees are highly engaged. That is huge!

If you consider yourself a Driver, don't be afraid to be appropriately nice. For example, when setting a challenging target, acknowledge the fact that the assignment will be demanding, but also offer support and inspiration.

On the other hand, if you're an Enhancer, try setting demanding goals meshed with sincere words of faith, confidence, and encouragement. In short, a balanced approach of both styles maximizes engagement.

For Managers

You want to bring out the best in your employees, but there's a fine line between being a tough manager with high expectations and being an over-demanding tyrant. If you have employees who are engaged and inspired, you'll have less need to be tough in your day-to-day management.

I personally believe managers should be more tactful and caring, because this builds an atmosphere of trust and a culture of goodwill - essentials for success. Tough, but nice, managers appreciate different work styles, give employees a sense of purpose, recognize good work, and treat employees with respect and dignity.

Finally, respected and caring leaders can ask their employees for extra effort when needed. I believe that, any employee would go to bat for their leader if they know the leader would do the same for them.

"Are Women Better Managers than Men"?

Dear Dave,

I know you won't answer this question, but I need to know what you think. My question is, do you believe women are better managers than men? There are many women in my office who read your column and this question is at the top of our list.

T

Dear T,

Trust me, I filed your question at the bottom of my "will not answer" list, but I decided to take a crack at this any way. Why do I feel like no matter what I write I am going to offend either men or women with my response? I am going to be careful here and write about what research has shown – that may keep me off the hook.

Management research

Leadership writers, Jack Zenger and Joseph Folkman studied 7,280 leaders in 2011. They looked at leaders in a variety of positions - from very senior management to lower level supervisors. In the study, they asked the employees of these leaders to rate these leaders in 16 leadership competencies including relationship building, team management, problem-solving, integrity and honesty, and change championing among others.

According to the data shared in the article, they found that women out-scored men in all but one of the 16 competencies surveyed, and in 12 of the 16, the women were better by a significant margin. And, in the words of Zenger and Folkman, "Two of the traits where women outscored men to the highest degree – 'taking initiative' and 'driving for results' have long been thought of as particularly male strengths."

This may surprise people who prefer a male boss to a female boss, but employees who work for female managers in the U.S. are more engaged than those who work for male managers according to Gallup research. Despite this Gallup finding, only one in three (33%) working Americans say they currently have a female boss.

Gallup also found that 41% of female managers are engaged at work, compared with 35% of male managers. In fact, female managers of every working-age generation are more engaged than their male counterparts, regardless of whether or not they have children in their household.

Gallup reveals female managers are more likely than male managers to encourage their employees' development, and they're also more inclined than their male counterparts to check in frequently on their employees' progress. Those who work for a female boss are 1.29 times more likely than those who work for a male boss to strongly agree their female boss tends to provide regular feedback to help their employees achieve their development goals.

My findings

The studies line up with my experience when doing an unscientific poll with people I know – both men and women. My sources candidly revealed that women: build better teams; they're more liked and respected as managers; they tend to be able to combine intuitive and logical thinking more seamlessly; they're more aware of the implications of the their own and others' actions; and they think more accurately about the resources needed to accomplish a given outcome.

Maybe women have to overcompensate and work harder because they are women in a male-dominated management world. This assumption was validated when I asked a friend of mine, a female manager, why women may be seen as better managers than men and she responded, "In order to get the same recognition and rewards, I need to do twice as much, never make a mistake, and constantly demonstrate my competence."

In conclusion, the study by Zenger and Folkman and the polling done by Gallup seem to demonstrate pretty strongly that women are seen as better leaders than men by those around them. However, what research shows doesn't amount to much if you are working for a boss – either a man or a woman – that you can't stand and is totally incompetent.

"Women Deal With Double Standards"

Dear Dave,

Where I work, women are encouraged to apply for upper level positions, but it seems like there are double standards for us women. We are told we can become leaders, but I still we are stereotyped as a gender that certainly does not have the leadership skills that men do. Am I being too sensitive?

M

Dear M,

No. You are not being too sensitive, because all too often you are correct. There are definitely double standards that inhibit the ability of women leaders to advance. This is my opinion.

One Rochester woman leader I know tells me, women are often perceived as too soft or too tough, but never just right, and as competent or likeable, but rarely both. However, one new study suggests a male leader is judged more harshly than a comparable female leader when they make an error – very interesting.

I also believe women are thought of as 'nice', so they must be nice even when they become leaders, which makes people believe they are not cut out for the role. However, if they're not nice, people wonder what's wrong with them. Men don't have this problem, because they're never expected to be 'nice'. Just kidding!.

Do Men Have the Leadership Edge?

The 'think leader, think male' paradigm may fade as people gradually begin to value those leadership skills that focus on relationships and results, and not just traditional leader traits that are more in line with masculinity.

Some theorists say that women have not been socialized to compete successfully in the world of men, and so they must be taught the skills their male counterparts have acquired naturally. But, at the same time, they must 'tone it down', or risk being labeled as being too assertive or aggressive.

Recent research led by Duke University's Fuqua School of Business, showed that top women, executives credited with responsibility for their own success, can be viewed simultaneously as more competent and more relationship-oriented than men, leading them to be perceived as more effective leaders than their male counterparts.

In business environments, even if women are thought to be sufficiently competent, they are frequently thought to be not very nice, but on the highest rungs of the corporate ladder, competence and niceness may have a certain level of compatibility for women top leaders.

Dealing With the Double Standards

What do women leaders do, then, in a world where image and perceptions matter, and gender stereotypes remain firmly entrenched? The answer is, women must be aware of stereotypes, but remain focused on competence and effectiveness.

Accordingly, some leadership experts believe women must understand how they are perceived and what role gender stereotype biases play in those perceptions. In short, women should be aware that these perceptions may exist, but I believe it would be prudent to not dwell on them by letting them dominate their thinking.

When encountering any double standards based on gender stereotypes, leading management thinkers advocate that women stay focused on their responsibilities, and not get sidetracked. Therefore, it is critical that followers see their women leaders as competent, determined, and strong.

In Conclusion:

Gender stereotypes misrepresent the true talents of women leaders and can potentially undermine women's contributions to organizations as well as their own advancement options.

Nevertheless, for leaders to be effective – men or women - followers must trust their ability to make difficult decisions, execute their initiatives, and act as positive, purposeful leaders.

"Good Leaders Get to Know Their Emotions"

Dear Dave,

My boss tells me I should never ever show any emotion at work. He says good managers hide their emotions and should not let feelings show, because it is a sign of weakness or a lack of control. I want to be more human with my employees and I think sometimes my emotions must show – especially when someone needs some consoling, or if I am just, plain mad at something. What are your thoughts?

N

Dear N,

There are times when you should be more stoic, calm, and straight-faced, and there are times when you should express some "controlled outrage." If, for example, someone has violated you and your integrity in a considerably damaging way, you have a right to express some "regulated" outrage.

I know there will be many reading this thinking Dave is advocating that rage is A-OK and we should pounce on people and things when we are mad – that is not the case. I am only saying that there are legitimate occasions when enough is enough and we need to make ourselves and our intentions clear.

However, being too emotional can create problems, but it can be far less of a problem than holding back all of your feelings. You may hide emotions in an attempt to stay in control and look strong, but doing so diminishes your control and weakens your capacity to connect and communicate with others. At the end of the day, business is a people thing.

Workplace Emotional Intelligence

Emotional Intelligence (EI) is something we all must master and possess at work and in our personal lives. Much is written about EI, but much is misunderstood about the practices and applications. EI is basically:

Being in touch with our emotions – know when you are irritated or angry. Be aware of those times and triggers that may cause you to want to rip into someone. Also, be sensitive to those things that bring you the most joy and satisfaction.

Demonstrating emotional control – I call this, basically, knowing when to bite your tongue and to "let things go." It is staying calm when others are losing control of their emotions.

This also means you are able to step back, take a breath, assess the situation, and act and respond accordingly.

Being tuned in to the emotions of others – If we are in touch with our emotions, we can probably be sensitive to the emotions of others, too. It means reading people and determining how they act and respond to things that may frustrate or irritate them. It also means knowing when empathy and compassion is most needed by others.

Building strong relationships – I can't say enough about this ability. This means taking the time to reach out and build rapport, bonds, trust, and respect. It means listening, showing emotional support, and managing any conflict that may arise, arriving at win-win solutions.

I think you should let your emotions out, and let people in. Both are critical to effective leadership. If you struggle with sharing your true feelings, it might help to know that people often don't show emotion, because they're not aware of what they're feeling, or they are frightened by what they are feeling.

Think about what you are thinking and determine what may be the best way to demonstrate what you are feeling at any given time. You might even be doing a good job of suppressing your anger or tempering your excitement now without even realizing it. If you are, you will be a good emotional role model for your employees. And your boss will come to realize that emotion is human and has a place in the workplace - if controlled.

"Grooming Future Leaders is Essential"

Dear Dave,

My company does a poor job of preparing people for leadership. People get rushed into jobs they are not prepared for and we often hire outside leaders, who do not know the company and, often, not what they are doing. Any advice?

M

Dear M,

Good question! Let me first say that, just as there are many managers who cannot lead, there are many leaders who cannot manage. Companies must groom managers as leaders - those who can get things done and also can lead and inspire his or her employees.

Defined, succession planning is a process for identifying and developing internal people with the potential to fill key business leadership positions in the company. Succession planning increases the availability of experienced and capable employees that are prepared to assume these roles as they become available.

The process of grooming new leaders for an organization is one that is done extremely well in some organizations and quite poorly, or not at all, in others. Succession planning should be a natural progression of training and developing for the next generation of leaders in an organization. Often the process is flawed either out of neglect, misunderstanding, or poor handling.

Reasons for succession planning

Succession planning is mandatory and some companies recruit and hire superior employees, develop their knowledge, skills, and abilities, and prepare them for advancement or promotion into ever more challenging roles.

Conversely, many companies believe their next generation talent is right under their roof – these companies probe their current talent pool and create a development plan for the resident stars. I believe you can do both – recruit outside talent and develop internal talent.

Because an organization expands, loses key employees, provides promotional opportunities, and increases sales, succession planning guarantees that the company has capable employees on hand, ready and waiting to fill new roles. The process should be developed and on the forefront of planning, instead of something managers think about only when someone is getting ready to retire or says, "Adios."

It's important to note that a succession planning process will also help a company retain superior employees, because these employees appreciate the time, attention, and development that the company is investing in them. Employees are motivated and engaged when they can see a career path for their continued growth and development.

Finally, I believe the need for effective succession planning increases at the higher, executive levels in any organization. With higher level managers, the skills needed are more critical and selection, as well as preparation, is much more demanding.

Where to begin

Good succession planning takes a lot of time and energy. William Rothwell of Penn State University is one of the recognized experts in succession planning. He provides a few key steps that need to be included in any succession planning process:

- o Clarify expectations for succession.
- o Establish competency models and measures.
- o Identify those with the potential to assume greater responsibility in the organization
- o Conduct individual assessments and assess individual potential.
- o Institute individual development plans.
- o Establish accountability for making the system work.
- o Evaluate the results.

A caution: While development plans and succession methods aren't promises, they are often communicated as such and can lead to frustration if they aren't realistic. Only give the promise of succession if there is a realistic chance of it happening.

I believe succession is a fundamental leadership process, because the highest calling for any leader is to grow the next generation of leaders.

"Leaders Need to Earn Employee Trust"

Dear Dave,

Most, but not all, of the managers at my place of work do not have the trust of their employees. I believe trust is crucial and I think managers need to earn trust. What suggestions

can you provide to managers to earn employee trust? I hope my manager will read your response.

D

Dear D,

I believe most managers think trust is an important factor in the business of managing people. But, trust is not a given - it has to be earned all day, every day. And managers don't do that just with their words – as important as they are – because employees watch their behavior, and base their opinions on what they see their managers do, not just what they say.

In most organizations, employees simply want to feel that they can believe what their managers say; that they will do what they say they will do; and that they will treat them fairly. For them, that's what trust is about. I think managers can be tough and demanding as long as they are fair.

Studies consistently show that lack of trust in management is one of the main reasons employees disengage from their work and seek jobs elsewhere. The problem is many employees are somewhat inclined to mistrust managers, often because of bad experiences with bosses at previous jobs.

This means managers can't demand respect and loyalty; they have to earn it. In the long run, it's difficult- if not impossible - to be an exceptional manager without employee trust. Employees are more likely to follow through on goals set by a manager they trust. I also think managers will never learn the truth about "what is really going on" unless they have their employees' trust.

Here are some tips for managers to build trust:

Be real - Be an authentic reflection of your organization's espoused (professed) values and principles while promoting transparency, fairness, and justice for all. And, don't play favorites!

Promote full participation - Make all employees feel like 'business owners' rather than robot observers. Show them that their voice matters, and that you truly value their input and that you listen to learn from them.

Develop your employees' potential - Help each individual feel like they are reaching their full potential and achieving their performance goals by encouraging and investing in their ongoing development.

Energize the culture - Create a positive, but realistic climate where your employees' energy is directed towards innovating, solving problems, overcoming obstacles, and fulfilling a greater purpose. I think people want to contribute and collaborate, so let them.

Empower employees to make decisions - When you show employees you trust their knowledge and skills, you allow them to make smart, appropriate decisions that benefit the company. And then, give credit - no one wants a manager who is a "glory hog.".

Make a connection - One of the most effective trust-building strategies is to create a personal and sincere connection. Do things that makes them believe you want to build and sustain meaningful relationships and that you are not just a hovering, pencil-pushing manipulator.

Be transparent and truthful - Share as much as you can about the current health and future goals of the company. Otherwise, you'll find yourself constantly battling the rumor mill. The truth is, if there is a void of information, employees are likely to fill it with imaginary, negative information.

Managers, in conclusion, the foundation for earning respect is establishing good relationships with your employees and by building trust within your teams and the organization. When employees have trust and feel trusted, they take stronger ownership of their work and seek new opportunities to grow in their roles.

"The Best Leaders Are Humble Leaders"

Dear Dave,

I hear so much about the need for leaders to be humble people and not brash, loud, and egotistical people. I agree with this. However, I do not want to come across as a wimp to my employees by being so humble they think I have no backbone. What do employees want to see in their leaders?

P

Dear P,

Great question. I, too, believe that humility and humbleness go along way when leading people. I also think we are all sick of the noisy, over-bearing tyrants that have been glorified in leadership history.

However, humble leaders must be engaging, effective leaders, who do have the strength and courage to encounter and deal with harsh realities. As I have pointed out in the past, the best managers are also great leaders, who possess and apply sound management skills *and* strong leadership approaches.

Leaders are selfless

A recent leadership study shows that leadership selfless behavior is one of four critical leadership factors for creating an environment where employees feel included, are excited about their work, and are truly engaged in contributing to the well-being and success of the company.

Selfless behavior was a style characterized by 1) acts of humility, such as learning from criticism and admitting mistakes); 2) empowering followers to learn and develop; 3) acts of courage, such as taking personal risks for the greater good; and 4) holding employees responsible for results.

Employees who perceived humble, selfless behavior from their managers also reported being more creative and innovative. Moreover, they were more outward-focused and reached out to help and support their colleagues above and beyond the call of duty. It appears that good role-modeling by managers rubbed off on the staff.

At Rockwell Automation, a leading provider of manufacturing automation, control, and information solutions, leaders are encouraged to be humble, sharing, open, and collaborative. In addition, leaders are developed and expected to be communicative learners that not only bring out the best in their employees, but also actively and constantly listen to employees to absorb what employees can teach them.

Here are some leadership guides for you taken from specific leadership development practices at Rockwell Automation:

Share your mistakes as teachable moments - When leaders passionately model their own quest for personal growth, they legitimize and encourage the growth and learning of others. Also, by admitting to their own imperfections, they make it okay for others to be imperfect, too. We all make errors, the key is to learn from them.

Engage in dialogue, not adversarial debates - Too often leaders are focused on persuasion and "winning" arguments. When people debate in this way, they become so focused on proving the merits of their own views that they miss out on the opportunity to learn about other points of view. Inclusive leaders are humble enough to suspend their own agendas and beliefs.

Embrace uncertainty - Ambiguity and uncertainty are common in today's business environment, but they must be embraced. When leaders humbly admit that they don't have all the answers, they provide opportunities for others to step forward and offer solutions. Also, employees bond when they work with each other to solve complex, vague problems.

Role model "Followership" – The best leaders empower others to lead. By doing so, leaders not only nurture employees' development, but they show trust and confidence in their employees. To grow, employees must experiment and experience.

A selfless leader is not a weak one. It takes substantial courage to practice humility in the ways described above, but the payoffs are developing involved and supportive employees, who can better lead when needed.

"Leadership in Tough Times"

Dear Dave,

I m a manager for a large company. Unless you live under a rock, we all know that organizations are having a rough time dealing with the current economy. I am finding it harder and harder to motivate my staff and make them feel better about the future of the organization. What advice can you give me?

C

Dear C,

You are correct! All kinds of strange things start happening when people have to face the stresses and changes turbulent environments produce. I, myself, try to stay patient, remain excited about my business challenges and expectations, and I view tough times as an opportunity to test my skills as a leader.

Accordingly, it is a manager's job to motivate folks and improve morale, even when the spirit of the troops is *'lower than a snake's belly in a wagon rut'* (I like that saying). However,

I know that effective leaders can stir up commitment and confidence despite the negative realities.

Where Do You Start?

First, as I always tell my MBA students, hire the best people to work for you. Surround yourself with a team of people who can fearlessly challenge your thinking and whose strengths make up for your deficits. These folks are wonderful for keeping things alive and fresh.

Next, be sure to communicate, often and authentically, with your employees. Because you're leading an organization through this downturn, you're undoubtedly introducing major changes — and inevitably encountering resistance to them. It's wise to engage with the resisters, learn from them, and alter your course if they suggest smart adjustments to your initiatives.

Naysayers are everywhere, but your biggest critics can be turned into your best advocates if you have the courage to listen carefully. Listening shows respect and, in turn, respect will be given back to you.

Motivation = Morale

Model the needed motivation. When a manager digs in and works hard – despite the odds – a strong signal is sent to their employees. Great leaders work harder to get through trying times, searching for more creative solutions and inspiring their coworkers to stay engaged.

I also believe that getting people involved in any way possible will increase their buy-in and create a sense of ownership in what is going on and how things are being handled. Otherwise, if things are just "thrust upon them," their natural tendency is to become defensive and resist.

Try to look for new opportunities that arise from the problems you are facing. Encourage your staff to be aware of opportunities for positive change. Again, this sends a strong signal that your employees are important and you count on their input and expertise.

This is huge: Make sure to recognize and reward your staff – even if means just offering a thank you for some work well done. One of the most basic rules of human behavior is that what gets rewarded gets repeated. Think creatively about how to recognize your staff.

Finally, the first and perhaps most important investment managers can make is to take an honest look at their own leadership. Take a look at the way you deal with employees, try to cultivate trusting relationships, and strengthen your bond with your employees.

In conclusion: Managers should tell employees everything they can about where the organization is headed; tell them what management and staff need to do to help the company weather the slowdown; ask for everyone's ideas to improve areas such as productivity, sales, and employee retention; and invite employees to discuss their fears and hopes.

"Leaders Should Listen Before Acting"

Dear Dave,

Our manager is a good person and means well, but he thinks he needs to have a quick answer for everything. It doesn't matter what the question or problem is, he chimes right in, before thinking about what is going on, or even fully understanding what the situation is. This has led to some mistakes. Please write something about managers that respond before listening.

T

Dear T,

Good leaders listen first, act second. It is not uncommon for leaders to act as your does – they feel the need and pressure to have a quick, prepared answer for everything. They also feel that, not having a quick response to everything may make them look weak or confused.

New leaders tend to make this mistake most. They think they must show they know everything about anything, so they jump right into the mix and start speaking before fully comprehending the lay of the land. They also try to establish their authority as soon as possible, and unfortunately, this is done by taking control of the dialogue.

No matter what level of management one has achieved, it's crucial to gain the respect of the employees – and this is done by listening before responding, or feeling the need to pounce on things right away. Employees want their leaders to give them a chance to speak and hear them out.

In addition, effective listening is a way of showing concern for employees, and that fosters cohesive bonds, commitment, and trust. Think about some of the most influential people you have known. I will bet these people had mastered the art of listening and keeping their mouth closed until they knew what they should know – and had something valuable to say.

Learning by listening

In practice, effective listening helps to resolve conflicts, build trust, inspire people, and strengthen teams. Research shows that employees choose poor communication as one of the biggest – if not the biggest – problems at their place of work. This often means information is neither shared with employees by managers, nor do managers listen to what employees have to say.

Communication theorists state that the three essential skills of listening, questioning, and responding are the backbone of discussion and dialogue. This means managers must master the art of being open and receptive to input, ideas, and feedback, ask good probing questions to draw people out and learn more, and then provide the response most appropriate to the given situation. In short, if you want to learn more, be interested in what people have to say and learn to ask better questions.

Many of us – and not just bad managers - spend a lot of time hearing (possibly), but little time listening. During the course of a conversation, we are reacting and talking, thinking about the next thing we are going to say, and then looking for an opportunity to say, Ooh. Ooh … listen to this." It is at this point, the other person starts thinking how futile the conversation is and checks out.

I know artful, engaging, and respectful listening takes patience and hard work. It is difficult to be quiet and not feel the need to assert yourself by talking before comprehending what others have to say. However, people will hear you out more if you first provide them the opportunity to speak and be heard.

True listeners not only build deeper relationships, they can build better solutions – because, they take the time to truly understand what is going on. Learning to take a breath before responding will definitely help you as a leader and will improve people's perception of you as a leader.

"Leadership is More than Charisma"

Dear Dave:

Our manager is nice enough, smart, and very outgoing and friendly. However, that is about where his talent comes to an end. His ability to lead to get things done is very poor. I think he was selected for his role, because he is liked, not because he is effective. Why does this happen?

P

Dear P,

Right away I can tell you that leaders must be intelligent, respected, and they must be effective in building bonds with their staff. However, they must also be more than just a charismatic "empty suit" that looks good in appearance, but falls way short in leading, guiding, motivating, and just plain taking care of business.

In many organizations, the most extroverted and intelligent member of a team is often chosen to be its leader. But these traits, even though we often perceive them to be requirements for leadership, don't come close to motivating staff, setting and attaining clear goals, thinking strategically, and guaranteeing effectiveness.

Yes, it pays to be smart and personable, but when leaders face a stressful situation - which tends to happen very frequently in every-day business environments – leaders must be analytical and responsive, while engaging and inspiring staff to achieve results.

More than window dressing

Leadership is not about position or a job title - it is about responsibility and action. It is about who leaders are and their behaviors, their deeds, how they treat others, how they make decisions, how they listen to others, how they accept responsibility for their actions, and how they hold themselves accountable. The best leaders realize that every action is a reflection of their character, integrity, and ability to be responsible and caring people – not just how they look or how persuasive they are.

So when choosing a leader, there are more important things for position search teams to consider than character traits and IQ scores, such as the demands of the position and whether or not the leader is a strategic and cultural fit and can perform as required. In short there must be substance and not just an appearance.

The problem with charismatic leaders is that their superb powers of persuasion make it easy for them to overcome resistance and opposition to a desired course of action. If your company is aligned and heading in the right direction, a charismatic leader will get you there faster. Unfortunately, if you're heading in the wrong direction, charisma will also get you there faster.

Whether or not someone will perform effectively in a leadership position is dependent on the setting and environment, the job demands, and the person's ability to develop and employ leadership skills. This cannot be predicted by neither their charisma nor their intelligence. It is determined by their ability to be cool and calm under crisis conditions and to rally the actions of staff to face and deal with adversity and reality.

Unfortunately, as I mentioned, we often choose our leaders based on traits such as extraversion, charisma, and intelligence (or perceived intelligence). And then we wonder why their performance does not live up to our expectations. In your case, you have a good person at the helm, but they are just inept in their ability to plan and rally support to execute their plans.

I believe that there is no substitute for responsible leadership that adheres to and honors high moral character and rules of conduct as guiding principles. To achieve this, leaders must be more than attractive, smiling people, who know how to work a room. They must be responsible, hard-working people who learn, adapt, and ... lead. At the end of the day, companies demand and need results – charisma, by itself, cannot meet this expectation.

"Leaders Cannot Make Everyone Happy"

Dear Dave,

We have a manager, who tries so hard to make everyone happy. Those of us who work extremely hard should be made happy, but there are some in our department who should be disciplined for their lousy work and poisonous attitude. I think our manager hates confrontations, so he operates this way. Thoughts?

P

Dear P,

Yup! That's a big "management avoidance" problem – avoiding acting like a responsible leader. The tendency to avoid conflict is natural. Most people want to be liked and unconsciously fear that arguments, disagreements, or negative messages will create tension with people they interact with on a daily basis

Unfortunately, the conflict-avoiding attitude backfires for managers and it's a huge barrier that often makes them appear weak and ineffective. A "make everyone happy" attitude can slow productivity, demotivate high performers, and lessen a leader's credibility. I believe good leaders face and address brutal realities, no matter how difficult they are.

A leader with a "make everyone happy" attitude can also be extremely detrimental to team morale. They may give poor performers a good review, because they don't want to have a confrontational conversation. Then, everyone gets rewarded - even people who aren't doing their job well…or at all.

I'm not saying that leaders should take pride in walking around confronting or firing people, but there are times they must do these things. Also, avoiding difficult decisions, crucial conversations, and other unpopular, but necessary actions, sends the wrong message to employees who will play on this management weakness and do even less work.

Manager avoidance motivations

So why do they do it? One answer is that some managers simply have no business managing people. Another reason is that they may be playing favorites. But in reality, the truth is probably closer to one of these following four possible motives:

1. Don't know where to begin – Analyzing employee actions and attitudes and who is or is not doing their work takes time, energy, and research. Many managers are not blessed with the skills needed to lead and employee confrontations and corrections are confusing and difficult to grasp.

2. Denial works, right? - Some managers think that if they keep quiet about the problems on their team the problems will go away. What they may not realize is that small problems can lead to large problems and things need to be taken care of fully and early.

3. Is much too busy – Because your boss is swamped, he may feel that any employee confrontation or intervention issues are not on his radar, and especially when he must attend endless meetings that achieve nothing. Sorry for that snarky remark.

4. Oblivious to the problem – Your boss may be doing the "head in the sand" routine, because he really doesn't seem to get that there's a problem at all. Truth is, there may be an issue that's affecting you, but for him it's not an issue, because … he can't or won't see it.

What you can do

If you believe you've sincerely tried to understand his motives for not acting on the needs of the work environment, then ask for a meeting with your manager to discuss how productivity is being hampered, because some people are not pulling their weight. Make sure to approach the discussion from a non-emotional standpoint.

And, if that doesn't work, you have a choice to either continue functioning within the confines of the current environment, or leave. If you choose to stay, work to control your own emotions and reactions to the avoidance problem.

"There are No Perfect Leaders"

Dear Dave,

My company offers leadership training, but it seems to me that there are no "perfect" leaders and everyone struggles to a large extent when trying to lead. What is the composition of the perfect leader and does he or she exist?

T

Dear T,

You asked the perfect question about the perfectly confusing and misunderstood art and science of leadership. To paraphrase W. Somerset Maugham, "There are three rules for creating good leaders. Unfortunately, no one knows what they are."

I believe there are no perfect leaders and that is why good leaders are always trying to improve themselves through self-study and self-awareness, training, education, mentorship, and making mistakes - and then learning from them.

What great leaders possess

Since there are no perfect leaders, it is difficult to build the "perfect" leadership model, which is why there are hundreds of them. However, I do know this: All great leaders clearly articulate and cast the vision of the future (answers the question, "where are we going?").

I also believe vision without a strategy to reach the vision is nonsense. Accordingly, great leaders possess the know-how to help the organization produce a strategy that will fulfill the vision. In addition, I believe great leaders get everyone involved in the strategic planning process, even if employees are only providing input about their work, their ideas, and their dreams.

We know that employee involvement and participation produces buy-in. Effective leaders have the ability to encourage and inspire employees to embrace and work through the many changes that are required to achieve the vision.

Change is scary to many. Why people resist change could fill a Funk and Wagnall's Encyclopedia (do they make those anymore?). Suffice it to say that, great leaders surface resistance early and often, so it can be discussed and addressed.

Strong leaders also possess a love of self-improvement for themselves and their employees. This trait makes them good coaches and mentors. Strong leaders know the value of continuous learning and live the quest for self-improvement. They also produce and provide vast opportunities for emerging leaders to develop their skills.

Great leaders empower their followers to get things by delegating the right work to the right people, and then trust them to get things done by getting off their backs. Although, some employees may deserve and need a fair measure of critical oversight, the practice should not be widespread – especially not for hard-working employees.

Leaders get busy

It is not enough for strong leaders to just rally their employees to produce greatness; they must also get into the trenches and dig into the nagging problems, as well as the opportunities for fulfillment of goals and objectives.

I'm not saying that the leader must – unless necessary - go to the production floor and start running machinery, but, they can go talk to their people and ask them what they see, what they need, and what could help the organization grow. They must be visible and be genuinely interested in the employees' work.

Every employee – because they are close to their work – has first-hand knowledge about what is working well or is functioning poorly. If we believe that big problems are made up of a lot of smaller problems, then – from a systems perspective – the smaller errors must be fixed. This isn't rocket surgery; it is smart leadership.

In summary, I believe great leaders are produced, not born to greatness. This means that leaders can and must learn those conceptual, people, and technical skills that will round out their effectiveness.

"Good Leaders Focus on Results and People"

Dear Dave:

The managers at my company have different opinions about how to achieve results. Some say you should focus on the work, production, and productivity and the desired outcomes will be achieved, while others believe that you should focus on the employees and their attitudes and they will bring you the results you need. Which is better?

P

Dear P,

The answer is … both. It's not a matter of performance or people, it's a matter of staff focus *and* a concern for results. Sadly, some leaders focus on neither. But, the best leaders produce engaged, happy, and well-trained employees, who can produce the results needed.

A study done in 2009 by management theorist, James Zenger bears this out. He surveyed 60,000 employees to identify how different characteristics of a leader combine to affect employee perceptions of whether the boss is a "great" leader or not. Two of the characteristics that Zenger examined were results focus and social skills.

Zenger found that if a leader was seen as being very strong on only a results focus, the chance of that leader being seen as a great leader was only 14%. He also found that if a leader was strong only on social skills, he or she was seen as a great leader even less of the time - a petty 12%.

Here's the biggie! The leaders who were strong in both results focus and in social skills, the likelihood of being seen as a great leader was astounding - 72%. Clearly, leaders who focus on both the tasks and the people doing them will have the greatest success.

A closer look

So, what exactly is the concern for people and concern for production (results) all about? It's important to note that managers tend to be more one than the other.

A concern for people is the degree to which a leader considers the needs of team members, their interests, and areas of personal development when deciding how best to accomplish a task. A leader with a high concern for people also talks to his or her employees regularly and nurtures a bond, demonstrating respect and sincere caring for staff

A concern for production is the degree to which a leader emphasizes goals, objectives, organizational efficiency, and maximized productivity when deciding how best to accomplish a task. This leader thrives on schedules, meeting goals, systems compliance, giving directions, and numbers.

Some leaders are very task-oriented (production); they simply want to get things done. Others are very people-oriented; they want people to be happy, empowered, and engaged. And others are a combination of the two. Again, sadly, some are neither.

Neither tendency is right or wrong, just as no one type of leadership style is best for all situations and all types of people. However, it's important to understand what your natural leadership tendencies are, so that you can then begin working on developing skills that you may be missing and to start integrating a concern for both tasks and the people into your everyday leadership style.

Unfortunately, employees are much more likely to be promoted to leadership positions, because of their technical competence and ability to be effective at the tasks related to job performance. We are thus promoting people who may lack the social and relationship-building skills needed to build teams and team bonds.

The solution to this problem lies in an integrated approach to the recruitment and hiring of leaders – or promotion of existing managers – who possess and demonstrate a balanced approach to leadership that meshes both a concern for people and a focus on productivity.

"The Most Important Leadership Skills"

Dear Dave,

I just came back from a 3-day leadership retreat and my head is spinning after seeing numerous models, charts, and diagrams about effective leadership. Is there any way to cut to the chase and find out the most important things leaders must know and practice?

K

Dear K,

The larger question may be: Is there a set of leadership skills fundamental to every management level within an organization? I believe all leaders need to use conceptual (thinking), relationship-building, and technical skills, but these skills vary in usage and importance as leaders climb up the ranks.

For instance, lower-level managers - those managing people closest to the tasks – may need to use a larger amount of techno-savvy as opposed to managers near the top of the organizational hierarchy. Conversely, managers at the top may need to use more conceptual skills than lower-level managers. But, don't get me wrong, all managers need to develop and use conceptual and relationship-building skills, as well as technological skills.

Leadership skills research

After years of extensive survey research, Zenger and Folkman (2011) have identified 16 core leadership competencies that have the greatest impact on a leader's success. Each survey respondent selected the top four competencies out of a list of 16 that were provided.

There was a remarkable consistency in the data about which skills were perceived as most important in all levels of the organization measured - the same competencies were selected as most important for the supervisors, middle managers, and senior managers alike.

It appears that truly exceptional leaders combine their competencies with the organization's needs and their own personal passions. The more these aspects overlap, the more exceptional the leader will be. The top 7 leadership skills (in order of importance) are:

- o Inspires and motivates others
- o Displays high integrity and honesty
- o Solves problems and analyzes issues
- o Drives for results
- o Communicates powerfully and prolifically
- o Collaborates and promotes teamwork
- o Builds relationships

As you can see from the results the most effective leaders are able to connect with and motivate people, while being able to problem solve and achieve necessary organizational outcomes. This means that the best leaders can think and act both in human terms and in strategic terms.

My personal leadership effectiveness list includes the following necessary skills:

Trust - Do your team members trust you? Do they accept that you will, without doubt, stand up for them whatever the situation? Only that kind of trust makes people feel empowered, gives them the courage to innovate, take risks, and to push themselves beyond their comfort zones to achieve success.

Empathy - Do you treat your team members as human beings, and not just as workers? I believe the best leaders are able to compassionately understand what their employees may be facing and try to put themselves in their shoes. Instead of pushing orders and directives at employees, the best leaders take time to draw out the emotions and obstacles employees face.

Mentorship - No matter how talented our employees may be, they still crave the motivating, guiding hand, the mentor can provide. When people are nervous and confused about what the future holds for their organizations and themselves, mentorship is critical.

And, Finally, Modeling the Way - Leaders create standards of excellence and then set an example for others to follow. They cut through red tape and clutter when it impedes action; they constantly clarify the path and destiny when people are unsure of where to go or how to get there; and they bring out the best in all employees.

"Leaders Model Excellent Behaviors and Attitudes"

Dear Dave,

Where I work, we have the opportunity to take leadership development classes. In one, we briefly touched on the need for leaders to be great role models, but we didn't explore it much further. Can you elaborate on the value of modeling the right behaviors and how someone can develop modeling skills?

P

Dear P,

Absolutely! When I think of modeling I think of living … living what you believe, embrace, and hold dear. We are attracted to leaders who live their values, beliefs, and principles in everyday actions and interactions with their employees. However, one could also model destructive behaviors, too.

There's hardly anything worse for company morale than leaders who say one thing and do another. A manager must accept their responsibility as a leader and serve as a role model by acting with engagement, commitment, consistency, and responsibility.

The value of leading by example

First, if leading by example is one of the best ways to motivate others, then leading by words that are negated by your actions is one of the most certain ways to bring out the worst in others.

When people witness leaders not living by their word, faith in the leadership is diminished. For example, if a leader expects people to speak respectfully to each other, they must speak respectfully to them.

Some of the best leadership advice I ever received was that loyalty and respect started with leading by example, such as truly caring about people, demonstrating integrity, continuously learning, setting and living high expectations and standards, making tough decisions, showing humility, and constantly communicating.

Learning to lead by example

Leaders establish principles concerning the way people (employees, peers, colleagues, and customers) should be treated and the way goals should be pursued. They create standards of excellence and then set an example for others to follow. The following suggestions should serve as good role modeling standards:

Show people the way – People are motivated by vision with a clear strategy to accomplish it. Not only should you cast a vision, but provide a roadmap to get there. Also, involve your staff as much as you can. If you state that their input matters, then get it, and use the best of what you learn from them.

Keep your word – If you promise something, keep that promise. You are only respected if you do what you say you will do. And, if you ask someone to do something, make sure you'd be willing to do it yourself.

Follow the rules - If you create and implement new rules for the office, then follow those rules just as closely as you expect everyone else to follow them. If you don't, you'll be seen as someone who lives a "do as I say, not as I do" philosophy.

Listen – This is so crucial. You want people to pay attention to each other, truly hear one another, and be open to all viewpoints, so you need to create that norm by demonstrating your own effective listening.

Walk your talk – Employees watch their leaders very closely, so If you state that it is important to stay late to get more work done (when necessary), then you must do it. Conversely, if you want your team to take some time to rest and relax, then you need to do it, too.

Leaders must be a role model of integrity and ethics, and modeling the way, is simply the leader saying and doing what he or she expects the followers to say and do.

"Working Under Fear"

Dear Dave,

My job used to be quite enjoyable and I felt good about the future and the strength of the organization. Lately, everyone is extremely nervous about their jobs and this has created a workplace where everyone is less trustful of each other and less happy about their work. I know I am just venting, but, what is happening?

B

Dear B,

Working in an environment of fear and uncertainty causes a lot of weird things to happen. First, everyone is spending way too much time practicing 'duck and cover' techniques. Second, employees feel so intimidated by the current realities that their fear is over-riding their ability to do their best work.

When a company leadership team's attention turns from "How can we do the right thing for our customers and employees?" to "How can we 'ride our employees like rented mules' at any cost?" then fear officially has a tight grip.

Employees who labor within a fear-oriented, command-and-control management environment are frequently 'motivated' (I should say 'driven') by threat and coercion. Not only does fear destroy any sense of team spirit and pride, but it also shuts down important communication channels, inhibiting the flow of creative, constructive, and corrective ideas.

The Signs Are Everywhere

The fearful employee worries that he/she will lose their job, be demoted, be denied salary increases, or be assigned menial tasks. Working in a constant backdrop of a fearful environment, the employee may become withdrawn, vengeful, depressed, abusive, or even violent.

According to one article I read on this situation, here are some signs of a fear-based workplace:

Distrust reigns - When employees have to stop and ask themselves, "Is it safe to tell Leonard my idea?" you have a fear problem in your organization.

Numbers rule and rules number in the thousands - An obsession with metrics, daily, weekly, and hourly, and a world view that says an employee is the sum of their numeric goals, are signs of a fear-based culture. Maybe the most stereotypical yet valid sign of a fear-based workplace is an overdependence on rules and policies in place of smart hiring, creativity, and common sense.

Management considers lateral communication suspect - Organizations that don't allow employees to brainstorm, mingle, and share ideas with one another are places where fear rules. People need to talk – they are people.

Information is hoarded - Cultures that allow people to hoard what they know to 'beef up' their power are cultures where fear has a lock. I praise the people who share what they have and know.

'Brown-nosers' rule - When the people who get rewarded and promoted are the least-knowledgeable, do the least, but are the experts at 'sucking up', fear has come to town.

CYA is the Rule - When getting through the day requires a focus on keeping one's head down, taking no risks, and staying out of management line-of-sight, your organization's soul – like Elvis – has left the building.

Management leads by fear - When leadership is based on keeping people in the dark and keeping them off-balance, no one benefits except the tier of managers near the top who justify their existence by devising ways to solidify their status. Even Machiavelli would cringe.

Managers must understand that fear-trampled employees don't do a thing for their business. Still, management by fear is a hard habit to break, because fear-whipped underlings don't squawk for fear of retribution. Meanwhile, your competitors may be hiring your best talent away and stealing market share, while you make it easy for them to do so.

"Leaders Need Motivation, Too"

Dear Dave,

I know it's important for leaders to motivate their employees. But, how can leaders stay motivated, themselves?

P

Dear P,

A leader definitely has to get and stay motivated; those who are not will quickly be seen as ineffective in their followers' eyes, as they expect their leaders to be engaged and enthusiastic about their work.

Basically, a leader's motivation comes in two forms: extrinsic and intrinsic. Extrinsic motivators come from the outside. For example, one reason that I teach college is that I need to make a living in order to survive. Intrinsic motivators come from within. For example, I teach college, because I get a great deal of satisfaction when I see students learn.

Good leaders try to get a balance of both motivators. Although many people believe that intrinsic motivators are the best, that is not necessarily so. Often, the extrinsic motivators lead us into new challenges and then our joy and satisfaction for doing it (intrinsic) are great rewards.

Managers Speak

I asked three managers/leaders how they get and stay motivated at work. Here are some things I heard:

One manager said, "Leaders are change agents who guide their followers onto new heights, while, along the way, they develop and grow their followers. A leader's two driving goals should be make the organization a success and that if the leader should leave, then she has enough trained and developed people to fulfill his or her shoes. These ambitions are what turn me on every single day."

Another remarked, "Leadership is like many other difficult skills - it takes practice. That is why it is important to develop leaders throughout your organization; although you can learn the knowledge and the skills in a short period of time, it takes plenty of practice to get it right. Senior leaders should always be coaching and mentoring their employees. It is quite motivating to know you are growing and developing your people for future leadership success."

Finally, one said, "I stay motivated by focusing on the problems and situations, and developing strategies to achieve lofty goals. And then by developing great people and giving them the means to accomplish a shared vision by ensuring that the necessary ingredients are there for organization success. In other words, my motivation comes from having 'goal directed visions' and then achieve them by inspiring my people to nurture change and address challenges."

My take on all this is that, the leaders I talked to were compelled by the natural and unselfish actions they do every day to grow their people and the organization. In short, what really motivates these leaders is the knowledge they are doing good by and with good people, who, in fact, will be leaders who carry on and teach these same motivations to other budding leaders.

Motivation Comes From Within

It is difficult to be turned on all day every day. Even great leaders probably have those days when they wake up and think, "I cannot believe the stuff I need to do today. How nice would it be to just roll over and go back to bed?"

But, the true leaders muster up the energy and determination to go out and do the right things, simply because they are the right things and they know are just the right people to do them. They turned on by tackling tough challenges and nagging problems. It also doesn't hurt if every so often someone says to them, "Nice job."

"Can Everyone Be a Leader?"

Dear Dave,

You always say anyone can become a leader. Is it really possible? Aren't there people whose traits make them unfit to be a leader?

T

Dear T,

Anyone can become a leader that has the willingness and drive to achieve goals in an ethical manner. Traits can be changed or reduced by focusing upon the more desirable traits and then using them to overpower the unhealthy ones.

This is one reason there are no perfect leaders — we all have a few unhealthy traits. But the better leaders concentrate on and grow their desirable, positive traits, so that they apply them effectively in challenging and stressful situations.

Right off the bat, I would say that selfish, brash, uncaring, and obtuse people will not be effective leaders. I think the best leaders are selfless, intelligent, personable, and know how to build relationships. To clarify, you do not need to be an Einstein to be a great leader, just a smart person who makes prudent decisions and actions.

Traits We Like to See

When I ask my MBA students what traits they most like to see in their leaders I hear repetitive themes: they want honest, humble, trustworthy, and strong, decisive leaders. They also want their leaders to be forward thinkers, who stay positive and do not blame and pass the buck.

Leadership books point to other valuable leadership traits such as determination, consistency, Emotional Intelligence, and an ability to reach out and help people when they need it. In short, followers want leaders who are reliable and care about them.

Traits We Hate to See

I am sitting at an airport as I write this and I asked a gentleman sitting next to me – who I had conversed with earlier - what leadership traits really turn him off. Without hesitation, he said he would never want a leader who is over-dominating, self-absorbed, and has no clue about what to do, or how to get other people to think and act.

He said he has had leaders that cared little for the employees and only sought to "move up" by looking good. He also told me that he believes some people just plain cannot be good leaders, because they lack the positive traits needed for success and possess all of the negative traits that only make employees stressed and frustrated.

My Beliefs

I think people can change and grow. I think everyone has the capacity to be a leader in given situations that require good people to step up and take care of things. You can be quiet, reserved, and introverted and still shine as a "Servant Leader," one who leads by serving others.

I also believe people will have epiphanies and "hit a bottom" of sorts where their ruthless or self-absorbed leadership behaviors will backfire and derail their professional and even their personal lives. It may be a type of leadership Karma where people will reap what they sew.

It is important to mention that some people just have not learned good leadership skills and thinking. They may have suffered under some dominating leader and accidently absorbed those same pathetic traits. Accordingly, what is learned can be unlearned, and these same people can learn and practice good leadership through education, practice, and solid mentoring.

In conclusion, leadership is more art than science – it's a people business and one that is enhanced by reaching out and helping those around you to succeed. People who cannot – or will not - build strong relationships will not succeed as leaders. The choice is theirs.

"What People Want in Their Leaders"

Dear Dave,

We are hiring a new manager for a very important position. The person who had the position was a failure and alienated everyone in her department. We have a good format for interviewing job candidates, but we want to focus specifically on leadership skills and need some direction. What do employees generally most want in their leaders? Any advice would help.

R

Dear R,

Leadership theorists, Kouzes and Posner, found that there are consistently four characteristics of admired leaders: Honest, forward-thinking, inspiring, and competent. The Gallup Corporation found that individuals expect four things from leaders: stability, trust, compassion and hope.

The Gallup study reflects the qualities people want their leaders to be and demonstrate through their actions. Stability is when the leader provides consistency and fortitude through challenging times. Hope is the leader's vision, positivity, and optimism for success. Trust is built by the leader's integrity, transparency, and honesty. Compassion is the knowledge that the leader cares for people.

Simply put, people want their leaders to give them what they need, so they can have confidence in the future. Whether you're leading a small team, or a major corporation, being a great leader means understanding people and what they need from you - and then delivering it.

Let's take a closer look at the Gallup findings:

Stability - To ensure stability, it's important that leaders look beyond the moment and consider what's coming down the road. This means reading the smoke signals and taking action early to shape the organization and equip it to respond and succeed in chaotic, turbulent times.

In addition, keeping employees informed is critical to stability. Information is empowering, and when employees are informed, they can anticipate change and plan accordingly. Employees are then less worried, less distracted, and more engaged.

Trust - Trust is at the heart of all positive relationships and trust has to be earned every day. Good leaders are authentic and sincere and demonstrate trust in their employees. And they build the ability to be trusted through words and actions. Again, communication is crucial and it's important to communicate transparently, honestly, and in a timely manner.

Compassion - Compassion is the emotion that we feel in response to the challenges of others that motivates a desire to reach out and help. To do this, leaders need to talk to and genuinely know their employees. They need to understand who they are and what matters most in their lives. Leaders need to actively listen when they share their concerns and respond with empathy … and actions.

Hope – I will first state that hope is not a strategy. However, in times of great change and turbulence, leaders inspire hope. I believe you inspire hope by clearly articulating a vision that motivates. Leaders must help employees see what the changes are, why they are needed, and what needs to be done – people need to see what roles they will play in change strategies.

Some feedback I have received from a management colleague is that, an effective leader is authentic, calm, consistent, caring, a good listener, and they remain true to their values. I'll add to this list by stating the most effective leaders show respect and can build bonds and relationships.

We all have different opinions on what is most important in our leaders, but one thing is certain … the culture is impacted, and in many ways created, by leaders at all levels of the organization. The best leaders are always thinking about the well-being of those they lead, not themselves.

"Signs You Are a Good Leader"

Dear Dave,

How do I know if I am a good leader? That's all I want to know?

B

Dear B,

First, I wish to quote three great thinkers to help you know.

Margaret Thatcher: "If you need to tell people you are the leader, you're not."

John Quincy Adam: "If your actions inspire others to dream more, learn more, do more and become more, you are a leader."

Walter Lippmann: "The final test of a leader is that he leaves behind him in other men the conviction and the will to carry on. The genius of a good leader is to leave behind him a situation which common sense, without the grace of genius, can deal with successfully."

Other Signs

I mention in my first book, "Ask Dave" (selfish book plug) that people follow leaders who try hard to care and show them respect, and I am sure your employees detect and respect your passion to become more effective at these very things. But, try as we may to become a better leader, the feedback telling us that we are doing well may not be so apparent.

So, what are the signs and how can we see them clearly? Here are some indicators I think you may find revealing of whether or not your leadership is effective:

Your employees want to learn from you – I think that when employees come to you for advice and knowledge, this is a very positive sign. It shows they respect your judgment, expertise, and ability to provide a focused, usable answer. In short, they see you as smart, approachable, and caring.

Your employees want to become leaders – The passion your employees have to become leaders may be a direct result of the positive leadership influence you have on them. They see you as a leader and it looks attractive and desirable. In short, they want what you have.

Your productivity and profits are sky high – Many call results such as profits and productivity bottom line measures. I see them differently: I see them as outcomes driven by excellent "top line" measures such as solid management, cohesive, collaborative cultures, and innovative mindsets and thinking. In short, great drivers, great results.

Your Opinions and Advice Seem to Matter – This means your peers, customers, and bosses see you as someone they can go to for the "straight scoop" on what should be done. You have been framed as what one of my management colleagues calls, a "go to" person, who is willing and able to provide some solid, rational thinking. In short, People respect your intellect and judgment.

Your Successes are Visible - When your small and large achievements are visible and appreciated, you can be sure your leadership talent is effective. I am not talking about only big monumental success stories, but even those small, incremental growth achievements that collectively lead to success. In short, your contributions matter.

I won't go into a dissertation of what the indicators of poor leadership are; I think we know from our personal experiences when bad leadership is present. I do believe that leaders may not always hear that they are doing great things, but they can sense that whatever they are doing is working for them.

In closing, we may not always know when we are appreciated as leaders, or that we are on top of our leadership game, but we do know when we are taking careless shortcuts and not doing "the right thing." Those measurements make it hard for us to sleep at night.

"Management and Leadership are Inseparable"

Dear Dave,

Several months ago, you described the difference between managers and leaders. I realize there are big differences between the two. At my company, I would describe the leadership as friendly and motivating, but what else would make me and my fellow managers more productive, positive, and influential?

M

Dear M,

The three things you mention – productive, positive, and influential – are absolutely key elements of great leadership. Meaning, productivity must take place or the firm will die, but achieving productivity in a positive and influential manner is critical.

Employees will perform if rewarded, but they will try to create excellence, if they feel they are important parts of an organization that treats them with respect and recognizes their contributions.

My passion – true leadership – is often absent in business and, sometimes, leadership techniques and skills may be learned and tried by managers, but as soon as a crisis pops up, managers throw their arms in their air, start screaming, "the sky is falling," and resort back to command and control management techniques.

Employees then become confused and the managers start thinking that leadership is only touch-feely gibberish, and they resort to thinking that the only way to get things done is by intimidation, fear, and manipulation.

I believe in three basic leadership structures that are very much evolutional in nature: Transactional Leadership, Transformational Leadership, and Transcendental Leadership. Think about this statement, "You can give people fish, or you can teach them how to fish." Or, you can teach people to teach other people how to fish!

Transactional Leadership is a transaction in progress. The leader defines what needs to be done, locates and trains/coaches the people to do what needs to be done, and then offers something (reward) for the employee doing the needed work. It is giving something for getting something.

You may question this as being only basic management, but it is leadership in the sense that a faith and trust is built between the leader and employee with the employee knowing that work done well will reap a valuable payoff in a timely and accurate manner.

Transformational Leadership takes things to a higher level. The leader actually transforms the thinking of the employee, causing the employee to feel a great sense of worth, contribution, and also to sense that they are a vital part of a purposeful mission to change and transform the organization.

The key difference between Transactional and Transformational Leadership is that Transformational Leadership creates and perpetuates within the employee a mindset of desire, an internal motivation to do things, and a need to contribute. The leader has taken the employee from a need for rewards only, to a covet for achievement and growth.

Transcendental means going beyond oneself. It is reaching out to help others learn, excel, and become more effective individuals. It means listening, teaching, sharing, and helping to "pull" people up and to help them be the best they can possibly be.

It is a true and unselfish desire within the leaders to make everyone around them successful and, by doing so, they become more successful themselves. By teaching people to teach and help others - and creating an environment of unbridled sharing - the leader gains power and accomplishes a great deal.

OK, the question you have for me, "Oh yeah Dave, just how do I do this if you're so smart!" My answer is: Discover what is really important to people. Find out what they want for growth and personal satisfaction and well-being. Deliver on these needs and you will be amazed.

Chapter 6 – Failure to Communicate

Whenever I see or hear about organizational problems that are caused by communications problems and issues, I am reminded of the famous line from the movie, "Cool Hand Luke," "What we have here is a failure to communicate."

I firmly believe that bad communication practices cause a majority of our work problems, not to mention the problems we face at home, or in our personal interactions with others outside of the workplace. Simply, we either pass along the wrong information, or we just fail to pass along valuable and correct information. Business thrives on communication.

We know that communication has matured and morphed over a relatively short period, changing from typical face-to-face dialogue to the use of innovative and sophisticated technology designed to increase efficiency and effectiveness. We now use technology such as email, text-messaging, social media, and video teleconferencing communication, which has made it easier to communicate, but has become much less personal, and consequently misunderstood. I believe we have traded effectiveness for efficiency.

We are people and we love to talk and, for a group of people to be an organization,, rather than just a random collection of individuals, they need to communicate with each other, understand what each other is doing, and coordinate their activities. You don't need to be a management expert to know that, the more effective the communication, the more efficient and productive the people and their activities will be. In addition, a well-organized workplace features openness and transparency throughout the levels of the company so that everyone is clear about his role and purpose at work and how it affects the work of others.

Good leaders know that, providing a culture of openness and interpersonal relationships will create an environment and culture of trust and the ability to shed dysfunction and the likelihood of people misunderstanding each other, thus providing a true ability to communicate amongst others at every level of the organization.

However, communications do not always function like a fine Swiss watch - all communication is complex and multidimensional with plenty of room for conflict and misunderstandings. For an organization to be successful, it must have all employees capable of sending and receiving information quickly, clearly, effectively, and accurately. Mistakes caused by miscommunication creates damage that is derailing, but hard to put a price tag on.

As I always say, leaders are responsible for communication to flow upward, downward, and across the organization. The "grapevine does a fairly good job of passing information and stories, but leaders must assess if what is being traded is accurate and if the truth is being spread around. Also, the smooth functioning of a workplace is dependent on cooperation between coworkers. In order to cooperate well, coworkers need to be able to communicate effectively.. Good communication must also exist within and between the team as a whole and the rest of the company.

Seasoned leaders understand that their jobs are much simpler when they hear and have access to a constant flow of information from their employees, as well as all stakeholders of the company - both positive and negative feedback, as well as ideas, observations, and problems should be sought out from every person in every corner of the organization. And, soliciting feedback from workers also improves staff morale by showing that management takes their opinions seriously and wants to include them in the ongoing improvement of the organization.

Let's take a look at some communication questions and problems and you can determine if my advice is sage and applicable.

"Hiding Behind E-Mails"

Dear Dave,

Why are people using e-mails to say things that should be said in person? I know that I am guilty of this, too. How can we get back to talking face to face and not use e-mail to vent?

T

Dear T,

Trust me, everyone is guilty of using e-mail to say things that are very private, very sensitive, and often, all too emotional and not well-thought-out. In short, face-to-face encounters are often difficult and require tact and diplomacy, and clicking-out an e-mail is simple and 'seemingly' non-confrontational.

I believe we all know that e-mail messages often do not clearly state our intent and meaning. What we achieve in message transmission efficiency we lose to a great extent in message clarity, purpose, sincerity, and significance.

Why E and Not Thee

I think that e-mail use is a modern extension of being passive-aggressive or, at least, avoiding conflict. Rather than confront an issue face to face, many employees today write an e-mail, even if the receiver's office is next to theirs.

Even though we know that the person(s) receiving the e-mail may not clearly understand what we are trying to say, or may even be upset with the message and by the way it is written, we send the e-mail message anyway, because we have the opportunity to cower behind the keyboard.

Often, sending quick, piercing, and sensitive messages is like throwing a spear at someone for some reason and realizing we can duck and hide for awhile while the person (spear receiver) is agonizing over the message. This is junior high thinking.

I asked one of my management colleagues why we use e-mails instead of discussing things face-to-face, and she stated that e-mail was designed so people could send out short, specific, informative alerts and messages, but have now become a means to send elaborate, complicated, detailed "War and Peace" dissertations, or drive-by, retaliatory message shootings at unsuspecting victims.

This means we can 'get things off of our plates' quickly and believe we have been absolutely effective in conveying our points, rants, and diatribes. However, we have all experienced being recipients of messages that take God knows how long to figure out and leave us fuming because we took things the wrong way … or did we?

E-Problems

The problem with e-mails is that most people aren't the best writers, so they are easily misunderstood, and can include nuances that the writer didn't intend. Yet once they're down in print, it's almost impossible to take them back. In a face-to-face conversation, you see if the other person understands your point, and you can explain it further if they don't.

It's also easier to turn someone down – or be turned down - in an impersonal e-mail, rather than in person; so if you really want someone's consent, ask them in person.

I advise my Rochester Augsburg College students to never to send an e-mail on important issues, unless the urgency is so demanding that you have no other options. I have gotten much better at writing short e-mail messages that make one clearly stated point and often ask for phone, or face-to-face dialogue to truly discuss the topic.

So what's the bottom line?

No matter what email application use and no matter what message you are trying to convey, unless you put appropriate discipline and boundaries in place when it comes to using this valuable communication tool, you're doing it wrong.

"Persuasion Can Be Learned"

Dear Dave,

I a am always so impressed when I hear persuasive people speak. It seems like some people just have a gift of persuasiveness. Can anyone become more persuasive? If so, how can I learn to be more persuasive?

S

Dear S,

Yes, persuasion skills can be learned. I hope I can persuade you of that fact. And, yes, some people appear to have that magical gift of persuasion, but, trust me, they have worked hard at developing the ability to persuade others.

As you have observed, being able to influence and persuade others to get them to do what you want them to do is a key skill not only in business, but in life as a whole. Simply, we only achieve real results through others and that takes effective and persuasive communication skills.

Persuasion Defined

Persuasion is influence and involves getting people to accept your arguments and/or point of view in a way that meets their needs. Others are motivated to accept your view, because they understand and agree, without sensing coercion or intimidation, or feeling they have been deceitfully manipulated.

According to most communication experts, persuasion can be defined as a symbolic process in which communicators try to convince other people to change their attitudes or behaviors regarding an issue through the transmission of a message in an atmosphere of free choice.

Whew! That is a mouthful. My Rochester management colleagues tell me persuasion is simply, building rapport with individuals; finding out exactly what they need; telling them how you will deliver solutions to their need(s); and then doing it. People become fully convinced when they believe that what is proposed is valuable to them and they have an opportunity to get it.

Learning Persuasion

Persuasion is mastery of several different traits. You need to be confident (not arrogant and brash), focused and self-assured (and not sound like a bumbling idiot), and be appealing and engaging (and not come off like a con artist). People want to hear rational, truthful, and credible messages from honest, sincere, and trustworthy people.

If you are dealing with people who are only inspired by facts and rational arguments, using straightforward logic is the best approach. However, convincing people through logic isn't the easiest thing and will require you to do a lot of research to be thoroughly prepared to present your case.

Also, emotional people – those hyper individuals who are all over the place when you talk to them – can calm down and focus on your message if you are calm and can support your discussion with credible and logical evidence.

Here are three key ingredients in presenting a persuasive message:

Know your facts - Be able to document any claims you make with factual data and information as proof. You've researched the evidence, so tell others what it says. But, don't come off as a "know-it-all."

Know your audience - What kinds of people are they? What is their current opinion on the issue or topic? How did they form their opinion? Where do they get their information? What are their own needs and interests? What arguments are most likely to persuade them?

Know how to fit the facts to your audience – Once you have your claims backed up by proof, and you know the interests and motivations of your listeners, carefully match what you have to say to what they want and need to hear.

How do you get to Carnegie Hall? Practice! The more you use rational persuasion principles the more influential you will become.

"Managers Must Talk to Their Employees"

Dear Dave,

Why do some managers not interact with their employees? Where I work, it seems like our managers tell us next to nothing about what is going on with the company. They don't even ask us how we are doing, or if we need anything. You always write about the need for managers to talk to employees. Can you please write something about this again?

R

Dear R,

Yes, organizations thrive on communication and dialogue. It is crucial that managers simply interact with employees, ask them questions about what is going on, and inquire into how they can help the employees in any way.

In addition, managers should pass along information about the company that will help employees understand the mission, vision, goals, and objectives pertaining to where the company is heading and what may lie ahead.

Some of my Rochester colleagues may not agree with me about the need to tell employees about the strategy and direction of the company, because they think it may confuse, overwhelm, or scare them, but I believe this organizational knowledge helps employees sense a "we-ness" in purpose and commitment, and inspires them to work toward shared goals.

Management By Walking About (MBWA)

If managers isolate themselves, their team may not learn from their experience, and this can undermine problem solving and decision making. Being connected can be a major factor for success - the more connected managers are, the better they can understand what motivates members of their team, analyze what's really going on, and find solutions that meet the needs of their people and their company.

When managers mingle and talk to employees – without smothering and pouncing on their staff – it shows that they care about what the employees are thinking and doing. Also, this "Walking About" provides opportunities for employees to ask crucial questions, or report errors and problems.

To get connected and stay connected, managers need to take time during their busy day, walk around and talk to their team, work alongside them, ask questions, and be there to help when needed.

When staff sees their manager as a person and not just a boss, they'll be more likely to tell them what's going on. Managers will get the chance to learn about issues before they become problems. Also, as the manager's team gets to know them better, they'll trust them more. They will be naturally inclined to share more information, and that will break down barriers to communication.

Talk Straight and Fast

Here's how managers can use conversation to help manage more effectively:

1) Talk straight - Be explicit, honest and authentic, especially when it comes to sharing bad news or addressing difficult topics.

2) Make talk happen - Stressful and challenging times can cause people to keep to themselves. Promote interactivity and encourage dialogue. Use less one-way communication channels (like e-mails) and choose mediums that allow for back-and-forth discussion instead.

3) Let everyone talk - Include people at all levels in the conversation. This will increase engagement among those who must carry out the most crucial every-day work.

4) Finally, do not shoot messengers - People will stop coming to management with important news, ideas, and input, if they fear they will be chastised for being some kind of trouble maker.

In summary, people are people, and they want to be talked to and treated like individuals that matter. When managers interact with their people every day, they learn a great deal more than sitting in their office with the door closed.

"Keeping an Open Mind for Possibilities"

Dear Dave,

Some people I work with are negative and closed-minded. It doesn't matter what idea is brought up, everyone seems to start coming up with reasons why it won't work, instead of discussing why it might. This is preventing people from bringing up ideas. What are your thoughts?

P

Dear P,

"The eye sees only what the mind is prepared to comprehend" ~ **Henri Bergson**

We know that, keeping an open mind is - in practice - a tough thing to practice. It means you are open to everyone and everything that comes your way, allowing yourself to embrace different possibilities, opportunities, people, views, suggestions, and interests.

Close-minded people essentially become negative and become shut off from the world of opportunities and possibilities. Their attitude makes them unwilling to try or accept anything else - this limits one's growth and experiencing new learning and discoveries.

Open-minded thinkers are receptive to new ideas and willing to consider other perspectives to see if they hold any value. They then can reject the bad ideas and embrace the good ones. Simply, the more you can openly consider ideas and listen to the people presenting them, the better you can think and make good, objective decisions.

Keeping an open mind also means to try and look at various approaches and ideas from different angles, and to assess what impact they may have, good or bad. It doesn't mean to believe or accept everything, but to listen, observe, and interpret, so you can comprehend every situation you encounter.

Opening Up

I tell my MBA students to be unbiased and broad-minded. Here are several ways you can model to your fellow employees the practice and importance of maintaining an open mind:

Comprehension – In meetings, try to understand, empathize, and make sense of someone else's situation, opinion, or stance. Learn to see things from his or her point of view. Keep in mind the history, education, experiences, and life circumstances of the other person.

Right or wrong – Even if you believe you are absolutely right, keep an open mind that you might be wrong after all. It is easy to become so polarized in our thinking that we shut out potentially advantageous views, simply because they were not ours.

Information - Be open to and process all information. Be interested in new, old, conflicting, and even strange insights – and don't shoot the messenger. Get the news and stay current on the facts by reading credible literature and news sources. Talk to people you would not normally talk to gain additional perspectives.

Ask great questions - Try asking sincere, open-ended questions (designed to encourage a full meaningful answer) to draw out what people are thinking, know, and firmly believe. Gain accurate insight by asking questions that probe and obtain what information is needed for everyone to fully understand the problems or challenges.

Be more alert - Listen to what people are really saying, or not saying, and pay more attention to what's going on around you. Ask yourself questions like: What dynamics are at work in various situations and why are they happening at this particular time? Why is someone saying what they are saying? What events have led up to a certain situation or condition?

Finally, try to deal with close-minded people rationally and calmly without emotionally coming unglued. Make an effort to see if you can help them become a little more open-minded without insulting them. I think every close-minded person can learn to be more objective and analytical.

"Before You Get Defensive, Take a Breath"

Dear Dave,

I have a self-management problem. I have developed a very defensive nature and I know I am overly-sensitive to what people are saying. I don't want to be the type of person who feels the need to retaliate whenever criticism is given to me. I really want to be more analytical and calm. Please give me some advice.

S

Dear S,

First let me say, that recognizing you have a problem is admirable and is the first step toward recovery. We all know people who would be defensive if you told them to have a nice day. I can hear it now, "What do you mean by that – don't you think I have nice days?"

236

Certainly not a day goes by that I don't have to deal with the defensiveness of others. I am sure this is the same for most people. When we get defensive we make it harder for others to understand what we're saying, and we usually make the other person defensive, too. Typically, conversations cease when one or both of the conversationalists become defensive.

In addition, defensive attitudes and behaviors stifle learning. In order to learn something new and to change, you need to let go of the old ways of thinking. This will never happen if we spend all of our time protecting positions that should be constantly and truthfully reevaluated. Smart, innovative people are adaptable and respond to new knowledge and patterns.

How to become less defensive

I believe we must be sensitive to our emotions and realize how our emotions affect our thinking. This requires some honest self-appraisal and soul-searching. We all know certain people or even events that will trigger defensive thinking, so we need to assess who these people are and what these events may mean to possibly jeopardizing cool, calm, and rational thinking.

Sadly, there are some people that like to enrage other people by jerking their "defensiveness chain." They find pleasure in seeing people get all upset when having to defend a belief or opinion. They know the levers that will make people defensive – they are masters at this. Avoid these people at all costs.

I believe that, after someone has said something that causes you to want to become defensive, these five steps can lead you toward non defensive thinking:

Take a deep breath - Think of the first thing you want to say or do and don't do that. Your first instinct may be to defend yourself against what you perceive as an attack, slight, or offense.

Take another breath - The second thing you want to say or do may be to retaliate, but that will only escalate matters. Don't do that, either.

Reflect and ponder - Think about the worth of the argument. Is it really that important? Is this one worth fighting? I believe an analysis of the value of the subject at hand will slow us down and allow us to respond appropriately.

Ask questions – Ask the other person why he or she is thinking they way they do? Ask for more information about the situation or point of view. Be genuinely curious and try ever so hard to appear open and in control of your emotions.

Focus on a solution or compromise – Defensiveness rarely produces action-oriented solutions. Try to think in terms of producing results and stay constructive. Propose ways and means to apply productive measures. Try to get everyone thinking creatively.

Finally, how do you get to Carnegie Hall? Practice! The more you do to stay in control of your emotions and look at things analytically, the better you will feel and the better you will communicate with others.

"Leaders Must Be Assertive"

Dear Dave,

I am a new manager. My problem is my lack of assertiveness. It's not that I don't want to be assertive, because I do. I am just afraid I may come off as over-bearing and controlling. How can I balance being assertive, while keeping the respect of my employees?

T

Dear T,

I think you are being assertive by writing to me. But, let me first say that, being assertive is one thing and pouncing on people and riding them like a rented mule is something else.

Let's see how the dictionary defines assertive. I found this definition: "confident, self-assured, and direct in behavior and communication without being pushy and annoying." I like that definition, because it states you can be purposed and direct without driving people bonkers (official business term).

I know people want to follow assertive leaders, not those who appear unsure, unsteady, wishy-washy, and cannot make a decision or define a direction. At least you know what pushy people think, but those who don't assert themselves (overly passive) miss the opportunity to share innovative ideas.

What assertiveness is and is not

Assertiveness shows conviction, reasoned purpose, and though-out intention. Aggressiveness on the other hand is often forceful and attacking, and may be emotionally injurious.

I believe you can be aggressive when pursuing goals or fighting diseases, but not when dealing with people.

Assertive leaders ensure that, ideas, opinions, and feelings are expressed in an open honest manner. They work on facts, not emotions, and they work to find a compromise or solution, while respecting the rights of everyone else.

Finally, assertive leaders act deliberately and decisively, and are able to manage potential or actual team conflict with reason and clear expectations. Leaders who are assertive work towards a win-win situation. This is in stark contrast to an aggressive leader who wants to win at any cost.

Learning Assertiveness

Assertiveness is one of those traits we expect to see in leaders and mastering assertiveness is learnable. If you find you are being either passive or aggressive, you need to work on the following skills to develop your assertiveness.

Self-value - Understand that your rights, thoughts, feelings, needs and desires are just as important as everyone else's, but remember they are not *more important* than anyone else's, either. Believe you deserve to be treated with respect and dignity at all times.

Express negative thoughts appropriately and in positive manner - I believe some appropriate and controlled "outrage" can be healthy and constructive. Allow yourself to be angry, but always be in control and respectful. Do say what's on your mind, but do it in a way that does not violate the other person's feelings.

Be confident - Use a firm, but pleasant, tone when speaking. When in a discussion, don't forget to listen and ask questions! It's important to understand the other person's point of view as well.

Learn to say "No" - Know your limits and what will cause you to feel taken advantage of. Know that you can't do everything or please everyone and learn to be OK with that. Go with what is right for you.

Being assertive means knowing where the fine line is between assertion and aggression. It means having a strong sense of yourself and being confident and decisive. And it means standing up for yourself even in the most difficult situations.

"Avoiding Decisions Means Avoiding Conflict"

Dear Dave,

We have a problem making decisions. My fellow managers avoid deciding on plans, changes, and you name it. We are slow to action, because of this decision avoidance, and we have missed deadlines and have let good opportunities get away. Any help?

P

Dear P,

Decision making is a key requirement for managers. However, commitment is difficult and requires people to proceed with real actions in real ways. This is challenging for many, because the complexity of the many problems encountered and the uncertainty of the possible decision outcomes make decision making a difficult, unpredictable, and scary process.

Most people would agree that great leaders are decisive. They make tough calls, and they have the backbone, positivity, and stamina to follow through. Research has shown that everyone experiences a sense of indecisiveness when contemplating a decision. But, decisive people are not swayed by indecision - once they make a decision, they become action-oriented and confident.

Decision psychology

Everyone knows that a company's planning and decision-making process often involves a lot of meetings, discussions, committees, task groups, etc., but very few hard-and-fast agreements. Often, the underlying problem isn't an inability to make decisions – it's a tendency to avoid conflict and – dare I say – the politics associated with decisions.

Because we all like certainty and are frightened by uncertainty, we often prevent decisions from being made altogether. In meetings, people may have doubts about ideas and directions, but they hesitate to openly express their disagreements during the discussion. But, when the real dialogue starts happening back in the offices, or in the hall, people may back-pedal and say, "Holy crap, we can't do that!"

Then, you have the other extreme, where some individuals are against anything and everything, and seek to stifle, derail, delay, or kill all ideas, suggestions, or changes. You may hear statements from these people including, "That'll never work" or, "You've got to be kidding me!" These people could depress a clown convention.

We know managers must be decisive, but this requirement is threatening to some managers. The fact is that managers are people and want to be liked – well, most anyway. They want others to think well of them and not feel that they're difficult to work with. They want to get along and seem like team players and not damage or destabilize relationships by appearing to be *too* decisive.

Another reason for decision avoidance is that many managers lack the skills to engage in analytical and strategic decision making. As a result, they are unable to engage in positive and constructive dialogue by defining the goals to be achieved, analyzing the facts, focusing on the core problem and opportunities, objectively listening to others, and then taking rhetoric to reality - problem-solving.

What to do

I think you should gather your fellow managers, and talk about decision making problems, processes, and practices. Be specific and discuss some real examples, how they played out – and should have played out - and the impact and consequences for the company and overall productivity. The focus should be on awareness and about the need to create decision-making process improvements.

Next, work with your colleagues to develop some ground rules and practices for constructive decision-making. Pinpoint and agree on how views and ideas will be shared, how issues will be addressed, how debate will be managed, and how consensus will be achieved.

Finally, take some time to really evaluate how you yourself make decisions. How and what do you model for others when decisions must be made? It is important that you set the tone by being analytical, decisive, and able to implement workable solutions.

"Get Tough Subjects Out in the Open"

Dear Dave,

It seems like people, especially the employees I work with, just don't say what they mean, or what should be said. My manager is the worst and seems to never honestly tell us how good or bad things are going. I hear a lot of wish-washy talk and I suppose this is because these people may be in denial of the truth. Am I wrong?

D

Dear D,

No, you are not wrong. I converse with many people - including managers - who seem to skirt the real issues, or try to avoid telling it like it is. I almost think they are convincing themselves that if they put bogus spins on things, or water down news to nonthreatening happy talk, nothing bad will ever happen, or ever happened.

All of us are critical of leaders who can't face the facts, but in truth, most of us engage in denial at one time or another, usually without knowing it. We all emphasize some things and

244

downplay others, based on past experiences, our personality, and our tolerance for discomfort. The fact is, denial is one of the most common defense mechanisms that we use to cope with difficult and uncomfortable situations.

However, great leaders tell it like it is. In other words, they focus on and define reality, no matter how painful or unpleasant it might be, and then move on to produce strategies to resolve problems or exploit opportunities. In contrast, less effective leaders sometimes avoid hard truths, manipulate the facts, and delay tough decisions.

Straight talk rules

To confront tough topics, I suggest that people find ways to encourage dialogue when complex issues are on the table. Denial is less likely to occur when teams look at the situation from multiple angles, challenge underlying assumptions, and construct a better, bigger picture of what's really going on.

Even the most open and honest of managers sometimes engage in "selective hearing" and interpret things the way they want them to be, instead of how they really are. That's why really good managers value the employees and colleagues who are not afraid to bring them bad news, report errors, tell them the truth, and help them see reality for what it is.

Given these challenges, here are two principles to keep in mind for dealing with denial in your work with colleagues:

Don't assume that everyone sees reality the same way you do - Facts and data are usually open to interpretation, and people have different underlying criteria for how they analyze and evaluate them. We all tend to capture concepts and situations with a different lens – often based on our personal bias. That is why good leaders are open to views, opinions, and perceptions, but are also careful to make sure everyone has a grip on the same reality.

Get tough subjects out in the open and on the table - Because of these different interpretations, try to find ways to facilitate and encourage dialogue, particularly when complex issues are scaring the pejeepers out of everyone. While denial can still occur, it is less likely when individuals and teams are able to look at the situation carefully, analytically, honestly, and thoroughly. You really can't solve problems until everyone has the same grasp of current realities – what I call, the "is."

In summary, denial is all too common in most organizations, which leads to delayed or inappropriate decisions, inaccurate or confusing communications, and misleading responses. But, it's important to remember that it's natural for people to avoid anxiety-provoking situations, which is why it's important for everyone – especially leadership - to help each other see the truth.

Chapter 7 – The Right People

I always tell my MBA students that, if they want to prevent problems in the first place and do amazing things, they must hire the best people they can find. If they have to trim money from other things, put the dollars into the people. Great people don't cost you money, they make you money.

In this economy, hiring the best people is more critical than ever. Managers can't afford to lose time, money, and results from a bad hiring choice. The cost of finding, interviewing, selecting, engaging and training new employees is a huge expense.

I won't get into any elongated rants about the less than ideal way we do hire people, but le me just say that, the interviewing and selection process is often a chore for busy employees and managers, who are thrust into the selection machine with a difficult to meet deadline. This causes all types of strange things to happen, such as efficiently hiring the best that are before you, instead of interviewing and selecting the best that are out there. It has become more science than art and a less than effective one at that.

We know that, hiring exceptionally qualified people frees up a leader's time and allows a leader to spend more time doing leader type things such as setting strategic directions and delegating, and then handing over incremental decisions to smart, capable team members. The trick is uncovering those talented and trustworthy people – and knowing what they look like when you find them. Good people can be delegated work and them empowered and trusted to successfully complete it.

I believe, and I have heard this repeated several times that, if companies managed financial assets, as well as the strategy and marketing needed to effectively do business, as carelessly as they do their valuable human assets, then shareholders would have their heads. Yet, although it is commonly accepted that individuals are crucial to an organization's success, many companies cannot assess, measure, or manage their employees' contributions to corporate value, nor bring in and develop the best talent needed to sustainably create excellence. In short, a company's future growth and competitiveness depend more than ever on attracting qualified workers and helping them work efficiently and collaboratively together within the organization.

In conclusion, an organization must utilize the resources it has available, or can find – even if they have to steal them - in order to have a chance at being sustainably successful. Without people, an organization has little to no chance of surviving, and because of this, it is important that the organization take special care to ensure that their employees, no matter how minor their role, are satisfied with their work environment, are fully engaged, and are being trained and developed to their fullest potential. People are the backbone of every organization and play a major role in the success or failure of an organization, regardless of what their job is within the company.

"Managers Don't Need Needy Employees"

Dear Dave,

I have a very needy employee. She's always looking for a pat on the head just for coming to work on time and an award for responding to emails. Also, she only talks about her problems and everything, of course, is wrong, and that everyone is against her. She is taking up all of my productive time. What can I do?

P

Dear P,

Having an employee who takes most of your time and is needy is a challenge. Their demand for constant attention can be tiring. In addition, you spend a great deal of your valuable time caring for them, which takes you away from other developmental management tasks.

No matter the industry or management level the problem of how to make sure that one high-maintenance employee does not zap your energy and keep you from assisting other employees, who also need attention, is far too common. This is basically a hiring problem and the wrong people were hired. It pays to check people out closer before hiring.

Needy people come in many shapes and colors. High maintenance, needy staff can range from those who need your continual "stroking" and approval to people who regularly make repeated mistakes – and don't learn from them - and from personalities that don't fit the team culture to people with dramatic personal issues that impact everyone around them.

You will recognize the "neediest" staff member by their endless rants, diatribes, and complaints around every aspect of their work, or their constant need to express dissatisfaction with management, coworkers, and the company in general. Those with low self-esteem tend to want to bring down the self-esteem of others.

These people can and do use their needy expertise to spread negativity within the team. You can easily hear their hallway conversations regarding how they are in a dead-end job, or how there is never a thank you given by management, or that, "communication around here stinks." They can rival leaches at sucking the life out of everyone.

Manager musts

For any manager, it is tempting to simply tell the needy employee to suck it up and get back to work. But, consider this: Not managing that needy employee and listening to the pleas means your other employees are paying the emotional and time-consuming price, because they have to put up with the rants. Passing the buck to staff causes your staff to be distracted from their work.

If an employee's neediness becomes disruptive, you may have to take firm action - don't allow a single worker to hold you and your workforce hostage. Explain the situation to the needy ones and let the employee know that, unless he or she is willing to take some responsibility for improving things, or just, plain taking care of business, you may have to begin disciplinary or termination procedures.

In all fairness, there are some needy people who do need their managers, but probably for reasons other than they realize. Managers should have structured conversations to try to get at the real issues. Maybe they don't have the right training, you haven't been clear to them about goals and roles, or they are suffering from mental health issues, and, therefore, they truly need some serious help. The only way to assess this is to sit down and speak to them.

Managing people is difficult. Period. There are personalities, emotions, needs, and then their personal lives to be dealt with. What makes a good manager a great one? One who can find the hidden talents in each of their people and help them grow as responsible and accountable individuals and team players.

"Great Job Candidates Have Many Great Traits"

Dear Dave,

At my company, we are very picky about the people we hire. We know what we want to see in job candidates, but what do managers absolutely not want to see in candidates? What traits, that a candidate may display, would turn them off the most and why?

D

Dear D,

Great questions! I went to some of my manager colleagues and asked these questions. But remember, different managers have varying views of what turns them on and off, and what they are willing to put up with, if the candidate has specific, technical job competencies.

Investing in talented and capable employees is critical for any corporation to continue to thrive. While you can teach a new employee the required technical skills, oftentimes it's the social and other behavioral skills that cannot be taught as easily.

What the Managers Think

The first thing I heard from the managers I talked to was that they always focus on whether or not the candidates have the job functional competencies, but they also look deeper to determine if the job candidates have Emotional Intelligence (to work and play well with others) and if the candidates are management material (are promotable).

This means, they look for both the job specific 'hard and soft' skills job candidates need. The following is the list of 'traits' the managers said they are most 'turned off' by.

Lack of Collaboration: An employee must be able to interact with others in a professional manner and be focused on collaboration … end of story.

Lack of Independence/Accountability: A new employee must also have the skills to complete work independently and display the ability to think, act, and make decisions timely on their own. If candidates seem to be unwilling to take accountability for their work and show confidence in their knowledge and skills, this sends a bad signal.

Detachment, Not Being Present in the Moment: Managers said, if the body is there, but the mind is in Pittsburgh (unless you are in Pittsburg), this is an absolute turn-off. They want candidates to be 'there', active, and alert to what is going on.

Aloof or Superior Attitude: It became evident that hiring managers believe a little humility and humbleness go a long way to presenting oneself. However, they wanted to see confidence without being elitist or over-bearing and – I like this word – 'uppity'.

Lack of Motivation/Commitment: Managers were turned off by individuals who do not appear to want to dig in and do their best work, and are not motivated to go the extra mile. Managers said they can tell when people are 'all talk with little action'.

Lack of Honesty/Respect: Managers said they are unimpressed if the candidates do not display honesty, sincerity, and integrity. They agreed they need to be able to trust their employees and know they are doing what is best for the corporation.

Lack of Adaptability: Managers said that the candidates must be open to change and be able to keep up in the business world today. The individual must demonstrate the ability to be responsive, agile, and bring forward fresh and innovative ideas.

Poor Listening Skills: Here is a biggie! All managers said that if the candidate lacks active listening skills and is constantly interrupting, or speaking without hearing and digesting what the managers are saying or asking, they '86' that application post haste.

In conclusion: Managers believe that if a candidate appears to be lazy, indifferent, above it all, and cannot commit and adapt, their entry point is the exit door.

"Mission Must Be Lived"

Dear Dave,

I think my organization has lost touch with what we do and what our purpose is. It seems like we just go through the paces and our zeal for doing what we do is gone. Once we were alive and spirited, and there was passion in our work. What I see now is people coming to work, putting in their time, and going home. Is there anything that will help us regain the spirit we once felt?

D

Dear D,

What we have here is a failure to communicate. Sorry, that line doesn't fit here, but I always wanted to use it. Now that I think about it, it does fit. Your employees are not communicating to each other the excitement, the emotions, and the love of the work and its meaning.

This is a culture problem caused by a lack of inspirational leadership on the part of your superiors. Either they have let this happen or they are oblivious to the condition. In any case, if someone does not feel the passion for their work, they will – as you say – just go through the paces and operate on auto-pilot.

Sadly, in these situations, you start hearing things like: "Why should I break my neck, nobody cares anyway." Or, "This used to be a fun place to work, but now it stinks." Or even, "I'm calling in sick tomorrow – I deserve it. You get my drift; people have replaced their desire with doing as little as possible.

What Passion Should Be

It's hard to put your finger on it (passion), but you know it when you see it. It's when people are going above and beyond the call of duty and there is a palpable vibrance as they interact with coworkers and customers. It's when things just get done and done well, and nobody had to force someone to do them.

Passion in the workplace is best displayed as excellence delivered, simply because the employees demand excellence, not mediocrity. It's when people reach out to help each other with tasks, or to teach them new things … simply, because they want to. It's when people stimulate and encourage each other. Finally– and I don't mean to be trite here – it's when there is a genuine sense of "we" and not "all about me."

Getting the Passion again

It will take a lot of work to turn the culture around, but it is up to every individual in the company to do their part to create a culture of desire. Passion must be driven by inspired, involved, and enthusiastic leaders. The transformation will require participation, engagement, and dedication, but the results are well worth it.

The best organizations hire and develop employees who are passionate about what they do, and those employees do whatever it takes to engage customers as well as each other. It sounds like your organization has the right employees, but they need a boost in their spirit of achievement.

So how can managers foster passion in the workplace? The Gallup organization has discovered that great workplaces:

1) Identify the strengths of all employees so employees get the opportunity to do what they do best

2) Hire people into the right jobs, so they can use their talents more often and more effectively

3) Hire great managers who are engaged and passionate about helping others discover their talents

4) Create an environment that encourages employees to become more engaged and passionate about their roles

Everybody has passion and management must find ways to activate that passion. That's why they call it leadership.

"Emotional Intelligence is a Mandatory Job Requirement"

Dear Dave,

My team needs to hire a new employee. We have been working on a list of qualifications and duties for the job description, including the need for the new hire to have

Emotional Intelligence. The problem is, we all seem to have different interpretations of what it is and we are unsure about determining if a job candidate has it. Any ideas?

R

Dear R,

Yes, plenty! I don't care what line of work someone is in, they will, at some time or other, interact with other people. Because of this fact, people need to be able to control their emotions and build relationships with others.

Most textbooks will define Emotional Intelligence (EI) as the ability to manage one's emotions as well as manage relationships with others. Simply put, we need to be aware of our emotions and ensure they do not override good judgment, rational thinking, and decision making.

We know EI it when we see it, but the question is, how do we probe and detect if people really have it and consistently display it. We rely on interviewing as a means of discovering the qualifications of others, so we need to craft great questions that draw out the truth of whether or not people are emotionally intelligent.

The 411 on EI

There are multiple aspects to emotional intelligence, but there are 3 constructs that we should zero in on most:

Self-awareness and self-regulation – This means the candidate understands the needs and wants that drive them and how they affect their behavior, and regulates their emotions so that any fear, anger, or anxiety experienced doesn't make them lose control.

Reading others and recognizing the impact of his or her behavior on them – This means the candidate has well-developed emotional and social "radar" and can sense how his or her words and actions influence their colleagues.

The ability to learn from mistakes – The candidate can acknowledge his or her mistakes, reflect critically upon them, and learn from them.

Detecting True Emotional Intelligence

According to Adele B. Lynn, conducting more interviews is not really the answer. What's needed are better interviews that measure a candidates' emotional intelligence.

To assess a candidate's self-awareness and ability to self-regulate, ask these questions:

Can you tell me about a time when your mood affected your performance, either negatively or positively?

Tell me about a conflict you had with a peer, direct report, or boss--how did it start and how did it get resolved?

To assess a candidate's ability to read others and measure the impact of their behavior, ask questions such as:

Tell me about a time when you did or said something that had a negative impact on a customer, peer, or direct report. How did you know the impact was negative?

Have you ever been in a business situation where you thought you needed to adjust your behavior? How did you know and what did you do?

To determine if the candidate can learn from their experiences, ask:

Have you ever been in a situation where you felt you needed to modify or change your behavior? How did you know? How have you been able to take lessons learned from that situation and apply them to another?

Tell me about a situation when you discovered that you were on the wrong course. How did you know? What did you do? What, if anything, did you learn from the experience?

The interview should be used to really listen and try to understand the candidate's experiences, successes, failures, and values, and then determine if this person could contribute to the organization and be emotionally intelligent when interacting with others.

Chapter 8 – Personal Problems and Challenges

People bring baggage to work. I am talking about emotions, bad experiences, bad attitudes, and stresses and concerns that are part of their personal life being brought to the workplace. I know it is hard to separate the "personal you" from the "work you." But, we are hired to perform and function well with our coworkers and management, not come to work and be a basket case of anger, disgust, frustration, and volatility.

Managers have it tough: They have to deal with both behavior problems and performance problems – which often comes as a package deal. Managers must knowing and recognize the difference and then seek to find a solution. However, one may cause the other – bad behaviors inhibit performance, and poor performance increases the likelihood of bad behaviors.

Employees have it tough, because they have personal problems that are chewing away at them, and this affects what they do, how they feel, and how they treat others at work. We are not robots – we think, we feel, we believe, and we communicate.

260

Everyone knows that, employees' personal lives often can affect their ability to do their jobs and interact with co-workers, managers and customers. Even when employees have serious personal issues to deal with at home, they are still must meet performance expectations and act professionally. This makes it tough for the employees that are suffering the brunt of some personal issues.

A common error made by new managers is that employee personal problems should be irrelevant to job performance and therefore something that managers can ignore – maybe it will just go away. We like to believe that when employees walk through the office door, all of their personal problems are left behind. Nothing could be further from the truth.

As much as we would like to believe that personal life doesn't impact a person's work, it very much does, and to great extremes. Workers dealing with problems at home often find their minds wandering, their attention is distorted, their clear thinking is hampered, and their emotions flair. Obviously, with all of this going on, they don't do their best work. Simply, Employees who are in pain — either physical or emotional — don't function as they should.

It's the manager's job to ensure employees are productive. But it's also their job to keep their employees motivated and balanced so that they will continue to be a contributing part of the organization. And to do that well, we all - coworkers and managers - have to know the employees as individuals, and to help them through some of the personal issues that interfere with their ability to do their best work. We have to spot our fellow workers, who may be in anguish, or are at least wrestling with some stressors that are making their life difficult. We can and should help each other. Let's take a look at some personal issues at work.

"Helping Coworker Build Self Confidence"

Dear Dave,

One of my employees is a really nice person, and works hard, but he lacks the self-confidence and self-esteem needed to move up in the company. I have asked him if he would want to be promoted and he said, yes. I know he is being held back and I feel bad for him. How can I help him?

D

Dear D,

Your heart is in the right place, but you have a big challenge ahead of you. I applaud your intentions and your unselfish desire to help this person – that shows true leadership.

We all know the best leaders have confidence in their abilities and this confidence is apparent to their employees. No one wants to work for someone who is unsure of themselves and appears weak in their ability to be decisive and determined.

Accordingly, those who should and do get promoted to management have high self-confidence and high self-efficacy (they believe they are effective). Business is tough and situations must be carefully analyzed and addressed with concrete, specific, and believable whole solutions. Confident leaders can do those things.

More About Self-Confidence

Self-confidence is a product of high self-esteem. In short, if you feel good about yourself, there is a great likelihood you will feel good about what you think and do. Conversely, if you believe you are weak or ineffective, you will have no faith in what you want to do. One feeds the other.

Self-esteem (defined) is the experience of being competent to cope with the basic challenges of life and of being worthy of happiness. It is confidence in our ability to think and reason. It is also confidence in our ability to learn, make appropriate choices and decisions, and handle change.

As a leader, you are, whether you like it or not, a role model. The higher your self-esteem, the more likely it is you'll be able inspire the best in others. Today, organizations want employees with knowledge and skills, and also those who possess self-reliance, self-trust, and the ability to trust one's judgment - in a word, self-esteem.

Helping to Build Self-Esteem

Realization – If possible and if applicable, you can start by providing easy access not only to the information he needs to do his job, but also, to information about the wider context in which he works - the goals and progress of the organization - so that he can understand how his activities help to fulfill the organization's overall mission and agenda.

Learning – Try to encourage and offer opportunities for continuous learning and upgrading of skills. Explain to him that your company is a learning organization and the learning he achieves will benefit the effectiveness of the whole company.

Recognition – When he does superior work or makes an excellent decision, invite him to explore how and why it happened. Do not limit yourself simply to praise. By asking appropriate questions, help raise his consciousness about what made the achievement possible, thereby increasing the likelihood that others like it will occur in the future.

Teach - Teach that errors and mistakes are opportunities for learning. Ask, "What can you learn from what happened?" This is a question that builds self-esteem, encourages self-assertiveness, expands consciousness, and may keep him from repeating mistakes that only lowers self-confidence.

In conclusion, you can help most by finding out what he would need in order to feel more in control of his work and, if possible, give it to him.

"No Room For Bored"

Dear Dave,

I'm bored and I'm so sick of the routine of going to work, day in, day out. It's not even that I really hate my job that much, it's just the routine of waking up every morning and spending my whole day in an office. When I'm there I count the hours until I get to leave. How does everybody else seem to work without being so bored?

R

Dear R,

You should just stop and think about how some people in the world have it worse than you and count your blessings. Yes, I know you are facing motivation challenges, but just think of how much worse you can have it.

Just about any person may feel like elements of their job, if not the entire job, has become boring. When this happens, your ability to perform your duties and interact professionally with others goes south – but, watch-out, your co-workers or customers might interpret your actions as laziness, resulting in career damage.

Find the Root Causes

I think the first step is to find out why you are so bored. By understanding why your job tends to become boring, you can help prevent these problems. Here are some common reasons that may apply to you.

No Challenge - When employees believe they are not challenged enough, they can become bored. Without stimulation, boredom can set in, especially if the duties of the job are repetitive.

Job Satisfaction - Another reason a job can become boring is that it no longer meets a worker's personal or professional expectations. Also, recognition is essential and, perhaps, you feel that your employer hasn't openly recognized your contributions enough.

Health Issues - Recurring or growing disinterest in your job can also be a symptom of a serious health problem, which requires medical attention as soon as possible.

What You Can Do

Methods you use to prevent boredom depend on your situation. For example, if you feel unchallenged at work, you might ask your employer for additional duties, or to be part of a different project more in line with your interests and career goals. Here are some more tips:

Look for the Good - Try to develop a positive attitude by looking for good elements in your boring job. Instead of focusing on what you don't like, think about what you do like and take enjoyment in those elements.

Innovate - Think about what specifically makes your job boring and look for ways to improve it. Whatever your specific situation, ask yourself what would make the job more tolerable and less boring. Then, talk to your manager to find out if there's a way to change things.

Challenge Yourself - If your job feels boring, because you're not interested in or knowledgeable about your field, learn more about it, so the job becomes more relevant to you. Again, you may want to ask about taking on additional responsibilities and tasks.

Note: This approach can also put you in a position of moving up to land more interesting, fulfilling roles.

Reach Out – Think about mentoring someone in the organization, or in your team, who could benefit from your expertise. Feeling fulfilled in this positive sense may help you find a sense of greater joy in your job.

In conclusion, work is work and it is not always glamorous and exciting. It's what we make of it and what we do while we are working that makes the difference between being engaged and going to sleep on the job.

"Finding the Right Company"

Dear Dave,

I need to find a new job. I am a manager and the company I work for does not treat me or anyone I work with very well. I don't want to get burned again, so I need some advice about what to look for in a future employer.

R

Dear R,

I fully understand and I, too, have worked for some companies that could mess up a one-car funeral. And, the management of these companies looked at employees as cogs in a machine – they were expendable.

The good news is that there are companies out there that treat their employees with respect and dignity, while helping them become the best they can be. These companies pride themselves on being productive places, where the employees are engaged and enjoy working there.

I was laid-off in the mid 80's. I remember to this day what one manager said as about 18 of us were being escorted out the door. He said, wherever you go, thoroughly check-out the culture of the company before taking the job. Simply, if the place is not a pleasant, rewarding, and engaging place to work, don't go there.

Research on outstanding companies

One recent study investigated 32 "exemplary" companies (collectively employing 600,000 people) across seven industries including hospitality, banking, manufacturing, and hospitals. At these companies, the engaged workers outnumber the actively disengaged ones by a 9:1 ratio.

The study also found several elements in place at the companies with "happy" employees, which are notably lacking in the others. What these companies do are things any company could do – the difference is, they do them.

First, the outstanding companies have involved, energetic, and curious leaders who want to improve. To be specific, leaders of great workplaces don't just talk about what they want to see in their staff – they model and practice it every day with their own teams. Continuous learners inspire continuous learners.

The best companies have leaders, who teach other leaders, to stretch and develop their employees, enhancing their natural capabilities. These leaders are educators and realize good people can become much greater employees with training and motivation.

The best companies ensure that employees know the company purpose, before expecting an inspiring mission to matter. This involves clear goals and roles. When employees know what is expected of them, have what they need to do their jobs, are good fits for their roles, and feel their managers support them, they will commit to what the company is trying to accomplish.

Outstanding companies trust, hold accountable, and consistently support their managers and teams. Strong teams are built when teams themselves size up the problems facing them and take a hands-on approach to solving them. Exemplary companies build staff capability and resilience, and gauge their effectiveness.

The best companies have a clear and comprehensive approach to performance management. The companies with the highest engagement levels recognize and reward their employees for good work. These companies use appropriate praise and recognition to develop and stretch employees to hit tough goals.

Finally, I believe great employers know how to prioritize and keep their eyes on the outcomes that need greater engagement to achieve. They help management and staff keep their "eye on the prize" and motivate them to achieve targets.

The thread that we see woven through these great practices is one of leadership understanding their people, engaging and motivating them, and providing them the know-how, resources, and tools to accomplish outstanding results. Any company that does these things is where you want to be.

"A Work-Life Balance is Crucial"

Dear Dave,

The amount of work we do and the extra hours we must put in are taking a toll on me and my employees. I want my employees to be happy, not burned out. The stress is becoming quite unbearable. How can we cope?

R

Dear R,

I understand. No matter how effective you are, work stress can take a toll. A work-life balance must be achieved, or even the most dedicated, driven worker will burn out.

The coveted work–life balance is a much-needed concept that involves proper prioritizing between "work" (career and ambition) and "lifestyle" (family, leisure, hobbies). We are not robots and need to "get a life" beyond our work.

I think that everyone struggles to find the right balance between work and life. As a manager, how you personally handle this challenge influences your team members - they are looking to you for signs of what they can and should do to achieve some balance.

What happened to balance?

You are not alone in the struggle to achieve a work-life balance. Throughout the world, many people are putting in extra hours, taking on extra tasks beyond their "job description," or using their computers and phones to be on call when they're not at work.

You need to ask yourself, is work a rewarding and fulfilling part of your life, or is it something that now takes up so much of your time and energy that you do not enjoy it? To make things worse, has modern technology made you so contactable that you can never take a breather?

I also believe that a lot of people are having a more difficult time finding balance in their lives, because there have been cutbacks or layoffs where they work. They're afraid it may happen to them, so they're working more and harder. Sadly, some managers take advantage of this fact and over-work people.

Here are some ways to bring a little more balance to your work week:

1. You need "me time" - When you plan your week, make sure to schedule time with your family and friends, be alone, or engage in activities that help you recharge.

2. Delete time and energy zappers - Many people waste their time on activities or even with negative, "gloom and doom" people that add no value. Take note of the activities that don't enhance your career or personal life, and minimize the time you spend on them.

3. Exercise - It's hard to make time – or find the motivation - for exercise when you have a jam-packed schedule, but it may ultimately help you get more done by boosting your energy level and ability to concentrate.

4. Try to Relax- Try leaving work earlier 1 night per week. Also, even during a hectic day, you can take 10 or 15 minutes to do something, like going for a short walk. Moving around a bit works wonders.

5. Innovate - Ask your employees about what they do to enhance their well-being beyond work. You may get some very creative ideas to help you "turn off" for a bit.

6: Ask For Direction - If you still can't seem to achieve some balance, it's time to be brave and ask your manager for help. Be objective and explain what the over-abundance of work is doing to you and your staff.

It is essential for each person make decisions based on what they truly want their lives to look like and then take the necessary actions to make it so. It's not always easy, but it can be done.

"Stand Out At Work"

Dear Dave,

At my company there is a "hiring pause," whatever that means, and the opportunities for promotion are slim. I work hard and I am looked upon as a reliable worker, but I know I just get lost in the herd and not stand out as someone who should be promoted. Do you have any tips on how to shine above the other workers?

S

Dear S,

For many people, the biggest challenge at work isn't trying to do the work well, for most of us the challenge at work is to get acknowledged -- to have the good work we're already doing get noticed by our superiors and coworkers.

As in your case, there are lots of benefits to being a standout at work, including greater potential for promotion, better assignments, and respect from peers and bosses. But, you nailed it; getting "lost in the herd" is an obstacle that must be overcome.

From Herd to Heard

Like your coworkers, you were hired to be a part of the company and a team, but folks can live in obscurity if nobody in upper management knows you exist. So, what changes can you make to separate yourself from the herd? Here are some recommendations:

Others and self - Outstanding employees spend a great deal of time reaching out and helping other people succeed: their employees and peers, their customers, and their suppliers. They know that their success and enhancing the success of others will lead to promotion and growth.

Work with purpose - Instead of dwelling on repetitive tasks that add little value – even though mundane things must get done, too – try to do something visibly productive for the company. For example: Take care of unresolved and nagging problems that people ignore. Also, volunteer wherever you can.

Proactive, not reactive - Be Proactive. Do not wait for things to happen and be a "reactive" employee. We all have had those moments where we know we could do more if we wanted to. Anticipate problems that might arise and come up with concrete suggestions to fix them.

First in, last out - Be the one who gets in early or stays late in order to get things done. Not only will your performance stand out, you'll also start to develop a reputation of reliability and dependability.

Develop a specific and unique expertise - Be known for something specific and highly useful – be the "expert" of something valuable to the company. Become the "go to" person- the person that can be counted on for help. But, know your limitations of what you really can and can't do.

Always offer solutions, not complaints – Anyone can complain, so try coming up with great ideas and prove how they can be implemented. Look at your own job and if you have a way it can be done more efficiently, then propose it. And, never bad mouth the company – speak well of the organization … as much as possible.

Rise above others - Be known as the employee who responds the quickest, acts responsibly, always follows up, or always reaches out to help others. Remember, the best way to stand out is to out-work everyone else. If you see that something needs to be done and nobody is doing it, do it.

When it comes time to promote, the management team is looking for a productive leader and they want individuals who are fully engaged in the company- those who care about their job and role, but also care about the business in its entirety.

"Learn What Stress Is Trying to Tell You"

Dear Dave,

I am a mid-level manager. Stress at work is ruling and ruining my life. I'm not alone. My team and my coworkers are in the same boat. It's affecting our work and the way we treat each other. I'll take any advice.

P

Dear P,

I understand. This may be easy for me to say, but try to change the way you think about stress. Seeing stress as a signal instead of a threat can help drive positive change.

When someone says, "My job is killing me" it may not be too far from the truth. Research shows our work environments have an impact on our mental and medical well-being. We also know that a stress filled workplace, or distressed workplace, can lead to the dysfunction or demise of an organization.

Stress management is more than just a 'feel good' concept. Stress has been called the "health epidemic of the 21st century" by the World Health Organization and is estimated to cost American businesses up to $300 billion a year.

Reflect on your stress

Identifying the triggers of stress will help you understand stress better. Ask yourself: What's causing this stress? If you're overwhelmed from the demands of a new project or task, take a closer look at why. If it is everyday pressure from a demanding boss, think about the motives and reasons why the pressure is on.

Further, are you unable to let go of some work that others could or should be doing? Meaning, are you struggling with delegating tasks to others? I think people have a hard time trusting others to perform and complete work if they feel only they can do that work best.

Taking charge of stress

There are ways you can reduce your overall stress levels and the stress you find on the job. Primarily, taking responsibility for improving your physical and emotional well-being is absolutely critical and you can avoid pitfalls by identifying knee jerk habits and negative attitudes that add to the stress you and your employees experience at work.

Here are some suggestions for reducing job stress, mainly achieved by prioritizing and organizing your responsibilities.

Balance your schedule - Analyze your schedule, responsibilities, and daily tasks and think about how they are affecting your well-being both at work and when you go home. Try to find a balance between work and family life, social activities and solitary pursuits, daily responsibilities and precious downtime.

Take breaks - Make sure to take short breaks throughout the day. Try to take a walk or find some quiet place to think nothing. Also try to get away from your desk for lunch. Stepping away from work to briefly relax and recharge will help you be more, not less, productive.

Prioritize tasks - Make a list of tasks you have to do, and achieve them in order of importance. If you have something particularly unpleasant to do, get it over with early. Also, break projects into small chunks. Focus on one manageable step at a time, rather than taking on everything at once and overwhelming yourself. And, don't over-commit yourself – I think, sometimes, you need to say no, or maybe later.

Emotional control - Emotional intelligence is the ability to manage and use your emotions in positive and constructive ways. Try to control your emotions and keep a grip even under the most challenging conditions – your colleagues may follow suit.

Finally, humor is crucial - There is no better stress reliever than a good laugh and nothing reduces stress quicker in the workplace than mutually shared humor. But, make sure the laughs are not at the expense of the feelings of others.

"Tell Your Story in Interviews"

Dear Dave,

It seems like every interview I have had has always been one where I never really get a chance to tell the interviewer(s) about the real me. The interview formats are all about the same asking me questions about challenging times and what I did, and the interviewers expect me to have a polished, well-rehearsed answer for these questions. How can I express the real me ... my past, my values, hopes, dreams, and aspirations?

K

Dear K,

Great question. I have interviewed many people over the years and I always gave the job candidates plenty of room to tell their story. Well-rehearsed and polished answers may not reflect the character of the candidate, nor their ability to think and determine what caused them to become the person they are today.

In that vein, I always tried to start job interviews with the same questions every time: Can you tell me about your life journey leading up to today? What got you here? Why is this role the right fit for you now and how have you prepared for it?

Often, I would hear the candidate explain their education, job history, and their service work – none of which tells me anything about their goals, personal revelations, assumptions, risks, and epiphanies. I could read their resume and understand what they are telling me. There is so much more they can relate.

It is at this point that I would tell them that I want to hear the details from their story that illustrate what drives them - their purpose, their mission – dare I say, their personal strategy.

Often, the job candidates looked at me like I was nuts and some even become tense and uneasy. Let me summarize this by saying that, few candidates have rehearsed a response to this line of inquiry.

Our story

The zillions of interview advice resources tell us that we should typically tell our professional stories beginning with our first job, then lock-step proceed into the next job, then the next … (snore). Again, the resume dictates our narrative. But, we need to probe deeper within ourselves and get at what drives us.

My Rochester management colleagues tell me that, your early years are critical to shaping your core values and authentic, imaginative, and untainted self. Your interests, how you spent your free time, and the activities and ideas you were drawn to provide signs of your purpose, passion for life, and what meaningful and fulfilling work you wish to do.

Go back in time

Interviewees should be allowed to reflect back on times when they were not defined by their job. How did they spend their time before they were inundated with work chores and became responsible for bringing home a paycheck? What were they drawn toward before they, their identity was defined by their "work self"?

Knowing where you were will help you determine where you should be going. Much of our thinking about our personal purpose in society is about reflecting on what made us who we are, and what battles we fought. Deep inside all of us are both battles scars and victories that have shaped us – we must be able to relate these stories in meaningful ways.

I'm not suggesting that you *not* be prepared to discuss your skills, abilities, and job-related capabilities. But, I do hope that the practice of rediscovering your early years will help you find and be able to articulate your purpose. These are the stories that should be told. I would ask interviewers if you could tell them.

"Dealing with Employee Betrayal"

Dear Dave,

I am a manager and I have always taken care of my employees. Without going into a long story, I was "stabbed in the back" by one of my employees. A confidence he and I shared was used against me, just so he could make himself look better. I am disheartened, because I never thought this would happen. It seems like maybe I cannot fully trust any of my employees now.

R

Dear R,

Please keep the faith! To be clear, trust influences every interaction in a working relationship and it strengthens bonds. Without trust, no relationship can thrive. I am sure you have other trustworthy employees, who deserve your trust.

Unfortunately, people don't always embrace and nurture trust the way that they should – it may be given freely at first, but then, it may be taken for granted. Sadly, your employee sought self-promotion versus living your shared pact of trust.

I think employees who backstab coworkers and bosses erode the company wellbeing as a whole. These individuals produce a culture of paranoia, jumpiness, mistrust, and negativity and the manager ends up spending most of his or hr day handling related conflicts.

The backstabbers

Backstabbing is a betrayal and it leaves scars - backstabbers "smile in your face," even after you treated them well as their manager. The motives for backstabbing usually stem from character flaws and a delusional belief that, the only way to get ahead is to stomp on people's hearts and trust.

Listen, it's all right to feel betrayed, but you shouldn't blame yourself for the incident. You do have every right to be angered and feel violated, but don't let your feelings deny trustworthy employees your faith in them.

Confronting the Backstabber

To begin with, I would swiftly meet with the backstabber. Calmly, but firmly, explain that you're aware of what he has done and that you're disappointed with how he has treated you. I would tell him what consequences his behavior had on your career. Be respectful, but be specific and direct. I believe open and honest confrontation is the only way to handle this deceptive behavior.

I always say you should be open-minded, so consider your employee's side of the story and consider any reasoning behind his actions – if there is any. For example, maybe he was coerced or pressured to betray you by threats and intimidation from another manager. Or maybe he failed to fully grasp the negative consequences his behavior would have on your job and respectability.

I know you really want an apology and a promise of no further backstabbing – and many may not agree with me – but, I would demand it. However, if you can, try to find forgiveness. If you can understand why your employee did what he did, and you don't believe he'll do it again, find a workable compromise, learn from the experience, and move on.

Keep in mind that, if your employee behaved in violation of company rules, review your company's policies to determine if you must discipline, or even fire him. If there is a violation of policy, provide appropriate verbal or written warnings and follow up to ensure your employee complies with stated expectations.

Finally, stay vigilant, but not jumpy, and know when and if you're being betrayed. Remember to get the facts and size up the situations before reacting. Employees watch their managers and are sensitive to their behaviors and attitude. They may not trust you unless you trust them first.

"Displaced Workers Need Help"

Dear Dave,

If loyal employees are laid off, what should and must a company do to fairly help these unfortunate individuals find work? Or, is it the chance an employee takes when they take a job and it is just to tough for them if their employment is terminated?

S

Dear S,

You could say that companies owe nothing to employees and it is "employment at will," meaning a person takes a chance when they take a job and there is always the likelihood they may lose it. In that vein, you are free to quit and they are free to let you go.

It seems like this is a bad deal when people put their livelihoods and family welfare on the line in taking a job for a particular company. It makes me think that nobody, but nobody, should take a job with a company that may be on shaky ground, has a history of sudden workforce reductions, or has had numerous management changes.

This also implies that you must take time to do deep research into the companies you are selecting for possible employment to make sure they are making money, or, at worst, that the company has helped terminated employees get back on their feet in some way.

What Some Companies Offer

Many companies offer a severance package of some kind to severed workers, I hate that term severed. Let's use the term, displaced workers. Of course, that even implies the employees were lost or left in a back alley somewhere. I digress, but that is my nature – sorry.

These displacement packages are explained upfront when an employee takes a job and can be viewed as a sort of benefit. It's sad to think an assistance package is viewed as a benevolent gesture by a company, and we should be pleased the organization creates that safeguard, because the organization's managers fear or know they may eventually mess up.

Displacement or what is also commonly termed "outplacement" packages include career coaching, stress management help, resume preparation assistance, and may even provide ex-employees with office space and a computer.

The company wants to give the employee the impression they have a sort of job to go to and, really, that job is looking for work. Rarely is this accommodation on the company's property, because, heaven forbid, they don't want the axed employee to think in any way, shape, or form that they are still a "part of the company."

These outplacement centers are staffed by savvy people, who have experience in getting people employed. Often, these job counselors are folks who have suffered through sudden termination themselves and they "feel the pain" of the recently laid-off worker.

This assistance is far better than somebody trying to work their way through the newspaper help wanted ads or the numerous Web job boards. Plus, misery loves company, and displaced workers are able to converse with other displaced workers and give each other tips. I am not sure if your city has these centers, but maybe it could become a hot biz opportunity.

So, Dave says, every worker should do their homework and check what is available for assistance at a company if one is unfortunately let go. Also, people should check the stability of the companies they apply at. And remember, pay may be an attractive part of a new job decision, but what good is a great salary if the job and the company are on shaky ground?

"Starting a New Job on the Right Foot"

Dear Dave,

I have been looking for a new job for quite some time and I finally landed what I think is the perfect job for me. I don't want to blow it by making mistakes that could be prevented. What advice do you have for me, so I start off on the right foot?

D

Dear D,

This is a great question, because I think many people start new jobs like they are trying to save the world – their enthusiasm and passion may supersede their need to first learn about the culture of their team and company, how things are really done, and what their job really entails.

Every company has methods and practices that are ingrained into the culture and systems. The employees are proud of the way they do things and have spent a lot of time developing their approach to their work. Also, they may be resistant to change and new ideas, so, when someone new comes into the company and starts spouting off about this is wrong, or that needs fixing, they are ... not very receptive.

When I was in marketing, we had a saying, "You're only new once." This means you have one opening opportunity to impress someone, so do it right. I believe people are most critical about other people, new ideas, or new processes early in their encounters with them. Their lasting judgment about things come from their initial contact and interaction with them.

The Right Foot

I suggest you start off as a serious learner and listen a lot more than you speak. Let people tell you about the processes and methods used and do not start telling people what is wrong and must be changed. Get a clear grasp of the way things are done, before presenting brilliant ideas.

Move carefully - Often people put far too much pressure on themselves to perform from day one. No one – least of all, your new boss – expects you to jump in and start solving major problems right away. Work hard, but don't try to save the planet.

Research Rule – Spend the first month finding out as much as you can about the organization, the mission, and the products and services. This can start before you assume the new job by browsing the company website and talking with people who know the organization well, such as former employees, customers, and suppliers.

Learn your job - Learn about your goals, what you need to get done, and the best way to go about it. This learning should generate additional questions, so never stop asking them. Learn your roles, responsibilities, accountabilities, and how you will be evaluated for your performance.

Learn the people - Learning who everybody is and what they do is crucial. This is true for the team with which you'll be working directly, and also for others who might hold more power than their positions seem to indicate. Try to make friends and create allies.

Beef up your skills – Prepare a list of the skills you'll need and use most for this position, and identify any that you need to develop or improve. Then plan how you'll learn the new skills that you need. You may want to seek out a mentor to help you.

Finally, it's not a sign of weakness to ask for help. If you don't know how or where to find the information you need, ask questions. Ask your boss or colleagues for help when you need it.

"Trying to Get the Passion Again"

Dear Dave,

At my company the love of the work and the passion for excellence has dried up. We all used to be so engaged and so excited about achievement, but now, we seem to show up, do our jobs, and cannot wait to go home. How can we regain the vigor and passion we once had?

K

Dear K,

You folks are facing a way too common dilemma that is occurring in many companies these days: people have lost their pizzazz and exuberance at work. The thrill of victory has been replaced by the agony of defeat (selfishly mutilated line from an old sports program).

I am not sure if companies have caused this loss of passion to happen, due to cost and people cutting, or the modern worker is just in it for the money and has become less enthused about their work. In any case, the outcome is not good.

The passion to work is correlated to the satisfaction you receive from your work. Why are so many people unsatisfied with their job? Many times people will say some variation of the following:

I don't get any recognition for the work I do (people crave appreciation).

My boss and/or coworkers are incompetent (may be true).

This job is a dead end (also a true possibility).

There are a lot of things you can't control about your job, but your attitude toward it isn't one of them. When you choose to do your job creatively, with integrity, and in a way that motivates others, you can find passion in your work.

Passion Matters

Rochester managers I know tell me they appreciate just how crucial that sense of passion is to worker creativity and productivity and, consequently, their ability to think up new approaches and innovations to spur the organization's growth and profitability.

I know that many of the most progressive and admired organizations today achieved their successes not through complex strategic plans, but because their leaders became passion catalysts by igniting a sense of passion and commitment within their employees.

The fact is, many of us are not only dispassionate about the work we do, but we often find ourselves shifting from being driven to consider innovative possibilities to one of defeatist and negative self-talk, frustration, and doubt.

Regaining the Passion

To begin, we need to figure out just what compels us to try to become the best we can be. Forbes Magazine writer, Amy Rees Anderson says we must ask ourselves these questions:

What is the passion that makes you want to jump out of bed in the morning ready to take on the world?

What is the passion that will help you keep going when everything around you appears to be falling apart?

What is the passion that will make you want to give 110 percent of yourself, rather than putting in the minimum requirement to pick up a paycheck?

Then, once we identify our passion, we can really begin to determine what pathways will allow us to pursue it. Also, knowing that the work we do is helping others is another important ingredient in feeling passionate about our job.

I believe that, while finding a job that is exciting can help many people to feel energetic, enthusiastic, and passionate about their career, the real trick is to find what excites you about your job each and every day.

"Boss Provides Some Workers Special Treatment"

I am sure my problem is not unique, but I wonder if you have any thoughts. My manager treats everyone differently and some, her pets, get treated a lot better than most of the staff. I hate to say this, but I am one of the people getting the most favorable treatment. But, I know it is wrong and I can see how poorly this special treatment affects those who are not receiving it. Any Advice?

N

Dear N,

Unfortunately, I know exactly what you mean and I applaud your ability to realize this "special treatment" is just plain wrong. Many people would just ignore this and suck up the favoritism your manager is showing.

Interestingly, one new study finds that workers feel better about themselves, are more willing to go above and beyond the call of duty, and are less likely to break the rules when they feel they are receiving preferential treatment from their manager. It appears that, if people have earned better, preferential treatment, productivity and well-being is increased.

So... the smartest managers can and should make everyone who deserves it feel like there's something special about them, while not creating resentment among all the other people. But any signs of blatant, unwarranted favoritism will have a negative effect on employee morale and behavior.

More Favoritism Research

The following survey was conducted by researchers at Georgetown University's McDonough School of Business. In polling senior executives at large U.S. corporations, they found:

92% have seen favoritism at play in employee promotions.

23% said they practiced favoritism themselves.

29% said their most recent promotion considered only a single candidate.

56% said when more than one candidate was considered, they already knew who they wanted to promote before deliberations.

96% report promoting the pre-selected individual.

Simply, if there's an open job, over half the time the boss has picked a favorite, and if they have, it's a given that the favorite is going to get it.

When You Are Not a Favorite

The advice offered by a Rochester manager I know, to those who are undeservedly ignored or rejected as a potential favorite, is to continue working hard, be professional, stay positive, and show you care about the company and your team. Your attitude and behavior speaks volumes and, ultimately and eventually, the best people rise in an organization – good organizations anyway.

Do some research and find out why others may be getting special treatment. It may be a friendship or some other relationship. Knowing this may help you determine whether it is fair or unfair favoritism. Take the time to consider if there are explanations or reasons that add insight and help ease your anxiety about workplace favoritism.

It's important to not be angry with the favored employees. It's usually not the employee's fault that he or she receives special treatment. So, don't blame them or mistreat them. I know it is difficult, but it is essential that you maintain a working relationship with the favored employee.

It is also important to figure out what qualities the favorites have that you are missing, and figure out what developmental things you may need in order to move forward in your career. I suggest you meet with your boss to map out a career plan for you, then, work hard to meet and exceed your goals

Managers: There's a risk that treating some employees better than the rest can turn others off. The key is to find the right balance - treat everyone well, but treat those whose work has been most productive with appropriate recognition.

Ω

David Conrad, Ed.D.:

Dave is Associate Professor of Business at Augsburg College and is Associate Director of the Augsburg MBA program.

He is also an independent business consultant working with companies in the areas of sales and marketing, management, and leadership development.

Before turning to a career in business education, Dave was successful in sales, marketing, and sales and marketing management for public and private companies in the wine and spirits, industrial, and medical supply industries for almost 30 years.

Dave has an Ed.D. in Leadership (organizational track) from Saint Mary's University of Minnesota, a Master's Degree in Management from Saint Mary's and a B.A. in Psychology from Winona State University.

His passion is teaching and helping people and organizations develop and succeed.